D1073009

Tell The Rock I'm Alive

C. BRANDON RIMMER

Published by
SUCCESSFUL LIVING, INC.
5624 LINCOLN DRIVE
EDINA, MN. 55436
In cooperation with
ARAGORN BOOKS Inc.

212 N. Orange · Glendale · California 91203

Published by
Successful Living, Inc.
5624 Lincoln Dr.
Edina, Mn. 55436
with

Aragorn Books, Inc.
212 North Orange Street
Glendale · California 91203

Dedicated to
Everett F. Harrison
Teacher, Counselor
and Brother

Books by C. Brandon Rimmer

HARRY

RELIGION IN SHREDS

MAYHEM & MERCY

With Bill Brown

THE UNPREDICTABLE WIND

Poetry by Donna Rimmer

The Greek writer Homer says that two old men sat on the wall of the city of Troy and watched preparations being made for a coming battle. Soldiers outside the wall were maintaining a siege and preparing to attack. Those inside the city were preparing to defend.

One of the old men turned to the other. "What a terrible waste of men and material. All they're fighting about is a woman."

The other old man agreed sagaciously, "They ought to give her back."

Just then, Helen, the object of the conversation, and the ostensible reason for the war, came tripping out of her boudoir and entered her garden. Both old men watched her as she picked some flowers.

In a minute or two, one turned to the other and said, "This war has got to go on."

That description of Helen is timeless. Each man who reads it paints his own picture in terms of his own culture and his own desires. Helen is described by the reaction men had to her when they saw her. This is the most eloquent kind of description.

It is interesting to note that this principle is

followed in the New Testament, particularly in the fourth Gospel, called the Gospel of John. The subject of the book is a man, Jesus, but there seems to be no physical description of this principal character. What the writer uses to picture Jesus is the reaction that people had to Him when they met Him. Jesus was a man who drew many people to Himself and repelled others. The writer of the Gospel gives us examples of both reactions and the reasons for them. The purpose of this present writing is to supply data that makes these reactions more significant. The data is both pictorial and historic.

It seems advisable, therefore, to say a word about the historicity of the Gospel we'll be using. The attitude of the scholarly world toward the Gospel of John has changed radically in recent years. A hundred years ago, it was fashionable to claim that this fourth Gospel was the last Gospel written and the date of its writing was about the third century after Christ. This position is no longer tenable.

Thanks to some great archeological work and to some great scholarship, John's Gospel is now reputed to be an early production of the Christian community. It is a matter of irony that the oldest extant fragment of the New Testament (P-39) known at this time is a passage from the fourth Gospel. It precedes the third century by many generations and is dated by some as early as A.D. 90. Suffice to say that this writer knows of no scholar, currently involved in the study of such manuscripts, who does not admit the possibility of this Gospel being the product of the generation that claims to have produced it.

Regardless of what you may believe about the credibility of the story in this book, faith in its historic origins has gradually increased among scholars, Christian and non-Christian alike.

One more thing. I've studied this book and taught from it for about twenty-five years. I believe that it is, indeed, "the greatest story ever told." This belief makes me a part of a very large group whose members are not limited by the boundaries of cultures nor by the lines between centuries.

The Baptizer

In the year 4 B.C., Herod the Great died. He had been the despotic and paranoic Roman ruler of the province loosely described as Palestine. In that same year a son was born to him by a Samaritan woman. This son is known in history as Herod Antipas. He survived his father due to his infancy. Several of the many sons of Herod the Great who had been old enough to pose a possible threat to their father's throne, had been conveniently and ruthlessly murdered.

Herod Antipas surfaced in Rome in his early twenties. He ranks among the great "con artists" of history. Unscrupulous, clever, but apparently attractive, he persuaded the Roman government to give him a portion of the land his father had once ruled. He was made tetrarch of Galilee.

While Herod was in Rome, two of his half-brothers who had survived their father's machinations were there also, Aristobulus and Philip. Philip married the daughter of Aristobulus, Herodias, a very beautiful woman. The fact that she was Philip's wife didn't bother Herod Antipas, and when he left Rome for Galilee he took Herodias with him.

It would be hard to image a ruler less acceptable to the Jews.* His ancestry was against him, his father had been Idumaean and his mother Samaritan, and the Jews hated Samaritans and Idumaeans more than any other people on the face of the earth. His marriage was against him. He was living in the kind of adultery that was most despicable to the followers of Moses for it was both adultery and consanguinity. Worst of all, he cooperated enthusiastically with the Roman occupation, with the Roman collection of taxes, and with the Roman idolatry. Except for a few Hebrews who (derisively called Herodians) supported him, he was universally hated. Because of him, Galilee seethed with incipient rebellion.

Herod was well aware of the opposition to him, and he knew that the main source of his problem and the main inspiration for his opposition came from the Jewish rulers in the temple, a group called the Sanhedrin. They hated him with a passion and they did all they could to cause him problems. He was looking avidly for anyone or anything that could help him undermine the influence of the Jewish leadership.

It was good news to Herod, therefore, when

*For the purposes of this book, as in much of the New Testament, Jew is a religious term only. Hebrew is the ethnic designation of a people.

he heard about a religious rival to the Jewish religious leaders. This rival was a strange preacher called John the Baptizer (not to be confused with John the disciple, the traditionally accepted author of the Gospel). The Baptizer was out in the desert preaching that the Messiah (Hebrew) or Christ (Greek), the biblically prophesied Jewish world ruler, was coming. "Therefore," preached John, "repent and be baptized for the remission of your sins."

He was a revivalist with a very potent message and he was forcefully preaching a concept whose hour had come. People flocked out to the desert to hear him. They went first by dozens, then by hundreds and then by thousands.

As might be expected, the temple rulers were understandably upset by the activity of this man, John the Baptizer. In the first place, there was the possibility that he was the Messiah. Whether he was or whether he wasn't, one thing was sure. He was undermining the importance of the temple. The religious rulers therefore sent a delegation of their authorities and lawyers out to the desert to "question" him. When the Baptizer saw them coming, he fired the opening blast. "You generation of vipers, who told you to flee from the wrath that is coming?"

This is not the normal way in which an "unordained," itinerant preacher greets an official delegation from the local ministerial association. Even less is it the way an "uneducated" Hebrew would normally speak to the august temple leaders. When news of this confrontation got back to Herod he was delighted, and he sent for John the Baptizer. John probably didn't want to go but when a Roman tetrarch sends Roman soldiers for you, you go. John went.

The ensuing meeting must have been a sight to behold. The contrast between two men could not have been more complete than the contrast between Herod and John. The tetrarch, surrounded by pomp and circumstances, by dozens of sycophants, and by the trappings of power, versus John. The Baptizer was in from the desert, burned and wind-blown, dressed in animal skins and showing on his lean face the marks of extreme devotion and extreme asceticism.

According to the text, John spoke first, and in loud, clear, bell-like tones, "It is not lawful for you to have your brother's wife." This is not the normal way in which one begins a conversation with one's king, and John was thrown in jail.

Outspokenness was only one of the reasons for his incarceration. There was also the matter of protective custody. The woman Herodias was still a member of Herod's court. She was not above murder, and Herod knew that a dead

John would do little for his political plans. Second, with John in the palace prison, Herod could see him whenever he wanted to do so. At the beginning of their conversations, John appealed to Herod, the way opposites sometimes do. Their conversations seem to have been frequent and prolonged. Herod used his considerable persuasive powers and all the pressures he could think of to try to enlist John's political support. He never succeeded. John never changed his witness, nor did he ease his condemnation of Herod's morals. The tetrarch's interest faded, and he would liked to have killed the Baptizer, but he was too sagacious to stir up unnecessary trouble with the people. John was considered a prophet and it's not smart for foreign kings to kill local prophets.

It is interesting that Herod's political sagacity was ultimately overcome by his lust. Herodias had a beautiful daughter by another man, a daughter in whom Herod had some interest. At a party in the palace, while John was still in prison, the daughter performed an erotic dance that so aroused Herod he promised her whatever she wanted. After a quick consultation with her mother, she asked Herod for the head of John the Baptizer on a platter. It would seem from this distance that it could have been her "payoff" to her mother for stealing her mother's lover.

Herod's lust was so strong that he did a politically stupid act and had John murdered.

The Baptizer had proved the uncompromising quality of his character by his incarceration and his death and this is important. But even more important is the fact that he had proven it by his life also. Many a man is willing to criticize the materialism and dissipation of his age and culture. But if he can afford to do so, he criticizes within the comforts provided by the society he's criticizing. (Some of the most bitter critics of the present-day American "scene" enjoy the greatest pleasures our materialistic emphasis provides.) Not so John the Baptizer, for he refused during his life to participate in any of the comforts that he could have enjoyed after his ministry was successful. Instead he continued to live in the desert, to clothe himself in the skins of animals and to exist on the food that the desert provided. As far as we know, he took nothing from any man.

Thoroughly dedicated men tend to draw other men to themselves and John the Baptizer was no exception. During his ministry he had a large number of disciples. Among them were two professional fishermen, one named Andrew, and a second who does not name himself, but who is identified later in the story as the John who wrote the fourth Gospel. These two men were with the Baptizer in the desert the day that Jesus made His appearance among those who were listening to John. They heard the Baptizer's testimony. This testimony was couched in the traditions of the time, customs that will have to be explained.

When a man assigned himself, or was assigned to a teacher as a student, he was not only a student but frequently a servant also. There was a great deal of menial work that could be required of him, but there was one thing he could not be asked to do. No teacher could ask a student-servant to untie the teacher's shoes nor take off his sandals. The Jewish opposition to idolatry was fanatical, and if one man took off another's shoes, he was bowing in a manner that, in the opinion of the Jews, should be reserved for God alone. John the Baptizer testified to Jesus by reversing this. "Here is someone whose shoelaces I am not worthy to untie."

Coming from a man of the Baptizer's integrity, these were startling words and the two fishermen were impressed. They ultimately became disciples of Jesus, and a great deal is known about them, but certain things can be deduced concerning them even at the beginning of the story.

First, they were professional fishermen, and if you have known many, you know that this speaks volumes in and of itself. The profession requires toil and courage. It also requires that a man be something of a gambler. A night of backbreaking labor can end in feast or famine.

The second thing of interest is that the courage shown in their choice of profession was matched by the courage shown in being willing to identify with John the Baptizer. Identifying with him would not gain any good marks for them in their temple nor would it help them gain friends in the business community in Jerusalem. Being disciples of John was no way to get ahead socially either. However, it did mark them as Jews loyal to the traditions of the prophets. They were men who were looking forward to the fulfillment of the prophecies concerning the coming of "The Coming One." They wanted to be part of the "new kingdom" from its inception, and they were willing to take whatever risks were necessary to keep themselves informed and in position.

Apparently the time had arrived, for the Baptizer had not only looked up to Jesus so much that he wouldn't consider himself worthy to untie His shoes, he had said one additional thing about Him, "Behold the Lamb of God."

To a first century Jew, this phrase meant a great deal. Andrew and John (later John the beloved) had been taken to the temple as young men. There they had watched their fathers buy a lamb for a sin offering. The animal had then been taken to a priest for inspection. The lamb could not fulfill the requirements of the law if it had any flaw or defect. When the inspections were over the sacrifice was taken into the temple and, there, hands were laid on it, committing to the animal the sins to be forgiven. Then the priest slit its throat. (The Mosaic code was clear, "Sin results in death.") It is understandable then that the phrase "Behold the Lamb of God" was far more meaningful to the Jewish mind than to ours. The Jewish mind had been trained by many years of Moses. Andrew and the young John had been thoroughly trained, and they were intrigued. It was quite understandable that when Jesus left the scene, they followed Him.

After some distance had been covered, Jesus turned around and addressed the two fishermen. "What do you want?"

"Teacher, where do you dwell?"

With typical Eastern indirectness his question had been answered by another question. If the fishermen had said, "We want to talk to you," it might have been an impertinence or an imposition. How would they know whether or not He wanted to talk to them? By asking Him where He dwelt they implied that they wanted to spend time with Him. (Otherwise, why would they want to know where He lived?)

Their question showed their intent but gave Jesus an opportunity to put them off if He wished to do so.

He didn't. "Come and see."

They followed Him and spent the evening in His presence. What this meant to them is revealed the next day in the testimony of Andrew. Remember, this was a tough-minded, professional fisherman, a Jew zealous for the future of Israel. A man turned slightly cynical by a rash of false Messiahs abroad in his day, yet after just one evening with Jesus, Andrew can go find his brother and say to him, "Simon, we have found Him. We have found the Messiah."

Simon didn't take his brother's word for it, nor can one blame him. He had Andrew take him to meet Jesus. Jesus looked at Simon as he approached and said, "You are Simon, son of John, but you shall be called Cephas." (Cephas is an Aramaic word meaning "rock" and Peter is its Greek equivalent. Therefore, the same man is called Cephas, Simon, Simon Peter, and Peter.)

There is a reasonable tradition that seems to fit the text. The tradition states that Simon Peter did not include himself among the disciples of John the Baptizer because of an unstable disposition and a violent temper. He felt himself unworthy. If this is true, the words of Jesus would have had tremendous impact. The one thing the man desperately wanted, stability of character, was here prophesied. It was prophesied with a power that Peter had never seen in a man before he saw it in Jesus. It hit him hard enough so that he abandoned his business for three years to trudge the dusty roads of Palestine. He wanted to stay in the shadow of the One who promised, "Your name will be Rock."

The next witness is a complete contrast to Peter. He is called Nathanael and he seems to have been a wealthy and devoted Jew. Let's put together a picture of him and his activities that contains much conjecture but does no violence to the text. If we assume certain things, the conversation between Jesus and Nathanael makes a great deal of sense.

Many houses in the Near East were built in the shape of a square with a courtyard in the center. Frequently, for the purposes of shade and coolness, as well as fruit, there was a fig tree planted in the courtyard. It was watered, when possible, by a pool. Nathanael retired to this shade in the middle of the day for his customary reflection and meditation on the Law and the prophets. Let us assume that he began his devotions with the Hebrew prayer that asks God for a "clean heart and a right spirit." We will assume also that the text of Scripture on his mind was the story of his ancestor, Jacob.

(In the book of Genesis, the first book in the

Hebrew Testament, there is a story about a man named Jacob who deceived his brother and had to flee for his life. He spent the first night of his odyssey sleeping in the desert with a rock for a pillow. Anyone who does this can be almost assured of light sleep and a dream. Jacob got his, and it's called "Jacob's ladder." He dreamed that heaven opened and he saw angels walking up and down a ladder between heaven and earth. From then on, to Jacob, that place where he had his dream was sacred and he built an altar to God there.)

Nathanael, like others whose fellowship with God was disciplined and therefore sometimes empty, prayed for an experience similar to his ancestor's. His meditation was interrupted by a servant who announced the arrival of his friend, Philip, a man from Bethsaida who had met Jesus.

After the usual salutations, Philip gave Nathanael the good news. "We have found Him of whom Moses and the Prophets wrote."

"Who is He?"

"Jesus, the son of Joseph, from Nazareth." Philip must have stumbled a little over the last word, Nazareth. That town in which Jesus grew to manhood seems to have been a "rest camp" for the Roman army. It had all the characteristics that such places have had since time immemorial. Every religious Jew like Nathanael hated the small city and everything in it.

"How could any good thing come out of Nazareth?"

Philip had but one good answer. He used it. "Come and see."

Nathanael went. When Jesus saw him approach He called out, "Behold Nathanael, a Jew in whom there is no deceitfulness."

Nathanael had been flattered before in his life. He smiled and asked, "How do you know me?"

Jesus said, "Before Philip called you, I saw you under your fig tree."

This was different. It may be that Philip hadn't had a chance to tell Jesus where he had found Nathanael, so how did Jesus know Nathanael had been under a fig tree? That is not the important point. Nathanael knew that the only basis for guilelessness was forgiveness. He knew to whom he had prayed. His smugness came down around his ears and crashed at his feet with his skepticism. He had done some research of his own on the nature of the coming Messiah, and regardless of what Philip thought about the ancestry of Jesus, Nathanael had his own idea. He addressed Jesus with the ultimate in praise.

"Teacher, You are the Son of God, You are the King of Israel."

Jesus was right about the guilelessness, and He smiled. Presented with evidence, Nathanael would go along. Jesus gave him more.

Nathanael had asked for an experience like his ancestor Jacob. Jesus said there was a new way open to heaven (Jesus Himself) and Nathanael wouldn't have to dream to see it. "You will see heaven open and the angels (messengers) of God ascending and descending on the Son of Man."

It is interesting that after Nathanael called Jesus the Son of God, Jesus called Himself the Son of Man. With Nathanael, there was no problem. Nathanael was a religious Jew and a student of the prophets who would know and understand the Messianic content of the term "Son of Man." The phrase meant more than it said, but it was a warning to Nathanael also. He was not to tell all that he knew, yet. The humanity of the Messiah was the means by which men were to be reached. The nature that lay undernearth that humanity was to be revealed in due time but not until certain things were accomplished. The answer Jesus gave Nathanael was both an assurance and a gentle rebuke.

So far in our story we have the following witnesses:

John the Baptizer, ascetic, devoted and martyred.

Andrew and John, professional fishermen who were willing to risk being known as disciples of John the Baptizer.

Philip, a sophisticated Hebrew, who lived and worked in the town of Bethsaida where there was business traffic with Gentiles, in a manner contrary to the Mosaic Law.

Simon, a passionate, violent man, soon to be called Peter, the rock.

Last but not least, **Nathanael,** religious, steeped in his Scripture and a lover of Israel, the true Israel of God.

These men are a study in contrasts so that together they may tell a story that they could not tell separately. But there's more to come. They are only the beginning of a parade.

Each from a different past
They came; a common life in Him to share
To follow the Christ, their lots were cast
His story to tell; His fate to bear.

As many streams unite and surge,
A powerful river's course to trace,
Their varied lives merged
In a flowing tide
To flood the whole earth's face

The Temple

The center of the Hebrew nation in general, and of Judaism in particular, was the temple. The center of the temple was the Holy of Holies, the ancient dwelling place of the Spirit of God in their midst. The Holy of Holies was separated from the Holy Place by a huge curtain. This center building, containing the Holy Place and the Holy of Holies, was surrounded by walled "courts" of varying degrees of sacredness depending upon their proximity to the center. The last court of all, the outer boundary of the temple property, was the court of the Gentiles.

In the original plan, the outer court, or court of the Gentiles was built for the purpose of proselytizing. It was here that Moses and the prophets were to be read and proclaimed to the Gentiles, that the Jews "might teach all nations." By the time Jesus entered the picture, the purpose of the outer court had been changed and the grounds desecrated.

Moses had commanded that those who lived away from Jerusalem should make a periodic pilgrimage to the temple for sacrifice. They were to "wrap their money in their hand" and go to Jerusalem and buy an offering to be sacrificed for their sins. The size of the offering depended upon the wealth of the individual. The most common sacrifice was the "lamb" previously mentioned.

The practice invited collusion and it soon came. It was not long before a worshiper knew that if he purchased his animal from a "certain" stall, it always passed the priest's inspection. It would be found to be "without blemish and without spot." The "certain" stall was one in which the temple authorities had an interest. Gradually the temple went into the business of raising and selling animals. (This is what the "shepherds who watched their flocks by night" were doing in the famous Christmas story. They were raising animals for the temple.) It was only a question of time until the stalls were moved into the temple property. (Who cared about converting Gentiles anyway?)

Soon the outer court was crowded with men doing business. Among them were the "money changers," for the money of Caesar, the denarius, had the image of Caesar stamped on it, and the Jewish law forbade any graven image. With this as an excuse, the temple officers profitably minted their own money to be used for tithes and for commerce. Tables were set up in the outer courtyard where the visitor to the temple could change his Roman money into that which was acceptable to the authorities. Needless to say that, while converting money, mistakes were made in addition and subtraction in favor of the "house." This led to understandable bickering.

What had been intended to be a quiet place of meditation and inquiry concerning the true God, had become a thriving, noisy, market place filled with bargaining, with shouting and with hustle and bustle. The grounds were so desecrated that the practice of walking around the temple to avoid crossing its grounds on secular business was abandoned. The shortest distance between two points in the city was the straightest possible line, and if that line ran through temple property, fine. It no longer mattered what a man was carrying, pushing or leading; through the courtyard he went. The scene was revolting to every good Jew.

We can speculate, because of a subsequent conversation, that one such godly Jew, Nicodemus, a teacher of the Law, was present when Jesus showed up in the temple. Jesus entered unobtrusively and quietly untethered the animals, large and small, that were staked out waiting to be sold. He formed a whip with the ropes, and with his back to a wall and his face toward an open gate, He started a stampede that cleared out the courtyard. Any tables that were still standing after the stampede, He kicked over, spilling the coins in the dirt.

This does not fit our traditional picture of Jesus, "meek and mild." We'd better start changing our picture to fit the story. There were temple soldiers hired to guard the money and the animals. There's nothing in the text about this being their day off. We might surmise that when they had taken a look at that face filled with indignation and righteous wrath and had listened to the whistle of the whip, they decided that prudence was the better part of valor. Possibly they busied themselves helping the others round up the scattered animals. As the dust settled and the bedlam receded into the distance, Jesus, whip in hand, approached the authorities who were still there.

"Clear out. This is my Father's house and you have made it a den of thieves."

He had just challenged the racket that was the number one source of temple wealth. These crooks were going to depart only if they had to, so they stuck around to argue. "By the right of what 'sign' do You do this?"

It was a stupid question. They had just seen prophecy fulfilled in front of their eyes. "Behold, the Lord whom you seek shall suddenly come to His temple. But who may abide the day of His coming, and who shall stand when He appeareth?"

The fulfilling of this Old Testament prophecy was the "sign." How can you have a "Sign for a sign"? If a policeman should ask me by what right I carried a driver's license with my picture and fingerprints on it, I don't know how I would answer him. A stupid question deserves an enigmatic answer.

"Destroy this temple and in three days I shall raise it up."

They were incensed. "Forty-six years it took us to build this temple, and You will raise it up in three days?"

The text says that He referred to His own body. This matter is discussed in greater detail in the fourth chapter of the Gospel, when Jesus is arguing with the Samaritan woman. Here, the enigma is allowed to remain; but the writer of the Gospel understood in retrospect. The temple was the dwelling place of God in the minds of the Jews. Jesus is saying that He is the dwelling place of God. The temple is now His body. Kill Him and in three days He will rise again. The significance of this conversation was lost on all present. Even the disciples, according to the text, didn't get the point until after they believed in the resurrection.

The significance of the cleansing of the temple, however, was another matter. Men who knew their Old Testament Scriptures knew that they had seen something which had been promised. Among those who felt its significance was a member of the ruling class, the teacher named above, Nicodemus. He had possibly witnessed the action in the temple, and that night he went to see Jesus.

Because it is written
His house shall be called a house of prayer,
Christ rose and went
To drive away
The unholy traffic thriving there.

Trampled in dust
The coins their true value realized.
The people fled,
No one could face
The love and pain in His knowing eyes.

Nicodemus

CHAPTER THREE

Much has been made of the fact that Nicodemus went to see Jesus by night. It is inferred from this that he was somehow cowardly. It would be better to say that he was practical. Those of us who have been objects of curiosity in the cities of the Near East know something of the inevitable, milling crowd of the idle curious. No one could have held a daytime conversation with Jesus that could have been in any way private or even comfortable. If Nicodemus wanted to talk he had to go at night. Furthermore, day or night, it wasn't cowardly. It was an act of considerable courage.

For the moment let us put ourselves back in the deep Southern part of the United States in the early 1920's. There is racial prejudice there now (and elsewhere), but in those days the lines between races were lines drawn with inexorable vengeance. Within our Southern context let us pretend that an itinerant minister, a black man, went to a small Southern town to preach. He preached with great power on the hypocrisy of nominal Christianity. If this little town had an all white seminary, and the president of this all white seminary went across the tracks and said to the black preacher, "Sir, we know that you are a man come from God . . ." he would have done something that under no circumstances could have been kept secret. News of what the white man had done and said would have been all over town the next day and the president of the seminary would have been looking for another job, or someplace else to put his seminary. Such open approval of a black man's ministry would not have been tolerated.

There was prejudice in Nicodemus' culture too. The difference between a Galilean peasant and a member of the Sanhedrin was greater by far than the difference between black and white in the southern United States in the twenties. Day or night, there was no way for Nicodemus to keep his visit a secret. As a ruler of the temple, he would make news if he sneezed twice, and gossip in the Near East travels faster than it does anywhere else in the world. His visit to Jesus was an act of courage, for by it Nicodemus put his neck on the block politically and religiously.

He had his reasons. If Jesus was to be the reformer Nicodemus hoped he would be, if Jesus could purify the rest of Judaism as He had purified the temple, Nicodemus wanted to help. If Jesus was more than a reformer, if He was the Messiah, Nicodemus wanted confirmation. Either way, the ruler could be of assistance. A young man like Jesus would lack political know-how and would need information about the Jerusalem situation that Nicodemus would be able to supply.

When they met, Nicodemus' opening statement was gracious. "We know that You are a man come from God. Nobody could do what You do unless God was with Him."

The answer he received borders on rudeness. We have to assume that Jesus spoke gently. "You know no such thing . . . No man can even see the kingdom of God until he is born again."

Jesus knew about Nicodemus' hopes and expectation, for they were universally believed among the faithful in Israel. The orthodox Jews hoped and expected that when the Messiah came he would give Rome "the boot" and restore Israel to power as a nation. Israel would be free once again. The remark of Jesus was related to what Nicodemus said, but not to what Nicodemus was planning to say. There must have been a moment's pause while Nicodemus recovered his poise.

"And just how is that supposed to happen? I'm an old man. How do I climb back into my mother's womb to be born again?"

Jesus shook His head. "No, flesh gives birth only to flesh. It is Spirit that gives birth to Spirit. You shouldn't be surprised because I said you must be born again."

There was silence while Nicodemus pondered the words. It is hard to shift from the concrete to the abstract. To Nicodemus the kingdom of God was a tangible, worldly thing. He thought of the kingdom in terms of David and of the prophets. An invisible kingdom left much to be desired.

The silence was broken by a gust of wind. In that part of the world gusts sometimes come unexpectedly. Jesus spoke again, "Nicodemus, do you hear that wind? You cannot tell from where it came nor do you know where it is going. That's the way it is with a man who is born again (or borne along) by the Spirit."

This is a beautiful play on words lost to us in English. One of the Greek words for wind is *pneuma*. It is also the word for spirit. Jesus is saying, you believe in the wind even though you don't actually see it, because you can see the effects of it. It is the same way with the Spirit of God. You cannot see it, but you can see the effects of it on men who have been influenced and moved by it.

This was very unsatisfactory to Nicodemus. He doubted that a kingdom based on something as ephemeral as wind was going to move the Romans out of Palestine. "How can this be?"

Jesus rebuked him, for had Nicodemus not been so interested in the visible manifestations of power, he would have been able to see the spiritual nature of God's work in his scriptural studies.

"How can a teacher of Israel, a famous teacher, not know these things? If you cannot see how God works in this world, how could you understand if I talked to you about how He works in the next?"

Let's paraphrase the words of Jesus in another context. If a man experiences tragedy in his life he can share it only with those who have a context in which the tragedy is meaningful. If a man's wife dies he seeks consolation for his sorrow only among his own kind. Can a man grieving over the death of a beloved marriage partner turn to his dog and say, "Fido, my wife died"?

The dog might bark in response because he was spoken to, the dog might even sense that something was wrong and wag his tail, but communication is incomplete without a common nature. If by some miracle, the man could put into his dog the characteristics of a human, what we loosely define as "human nature," he might be able to communicate something of his sorrow and sense of loss. Until this is done, there will be very little intelligent conversation.

This is the problem God faces, the problem Jesus is talking about to Nicodemus. How does God communicate with man? He can't, for man does not share His nature. Being born again is the process by which He places something of

His own nature within man. When, in a very limited sense, something of the nature of God has been placed within man, conversation on a very limited scale begins. Until that moment meaningful communication is inhibited by restrictions of the "flesh."

Jesus meant more by "flesh" than physical body. He used the term to stand for all that a person is at birth. The concept of being born again is that the nature of God, the nature of Spirit, comes in from the outside as does the first nature which is the product of our parents. Our second birth and our second nature are the product of God and of God's Spirit.

Assuming all this to be true, how does it solve the problem for Nicodemus? His question in one sense is still not answered. What is the source of the second birth? How and why is it begun?

Jesus turns the thinking of Nicodemus back to the Jewish Scripture. "As Moses lifted the serpent in the wilderness, so must the Son of Man be lifted up."

To try to get at some of the meaning let's look at the story to which Jesus is making reference. It's in the second book of the Hebrew Scriptures. It's called "Exodus." In it the Jews, or Israelites, leave Egypt where they had been slaves and enter the wilderness on their way to Canaan, "the promised land." After a period of time, the wilderness experience got "old."

The food was monotonous, the water brackish and the weather miserable. The possibility of going back to Egypt became more and more attractive. From a distance, slavery in Egypt began to look better and better.

A revolt took place against their leader, Moses. Many of the Israelites began to go back to Egypt and to slavery. According to the story, God sent snakes among the Israelites that were poisonous. People who were bitten began to die.

The presence of death affects value judgments. Remember the famous story about the sinking of the trans-Atlantic ocean liner, the Titanic? While the icy sea was slowly rising around the ship the passengers didn't sing a song along the lines of "The merry-go-round broke down." Something quite different came to mind, and men and women who probably hadn't given the concept of God a thought during the preceding hours, days, weeks or months, suddenly remembered the words and music of a hymn that was almost universally known in their culture at that time. They sang, "Nearer My God to Thee."

According to the Mosaic story, the Israelites suddenly faced reality. Reality is this: Slave or free, wilderness or Egypt, people still die. The people started screaming to Moses to intervene with God and save their lives. Moses did intercede. God gave him peculiar instructions. According to the Old Testament, Moses was told to make an image of the serpents, hang it on a pole, and lift it high. Whoever looked "on" it would live.

We won't get the point until we realize that there are two ways to "look" or to "see." One is physical vision. The other is "see" in the sense to understand. A teacher may say to a class concerning a problem solved for them on the blackboard, "Now do you see it?" The teacher means, "Do you understand?"

In the Exodus story, God says to Moses that whoever looks and sees, or understands, will live. In other words, a curse could bring a blessing. Because of the snakes, they were no longer concerned with Egypt and returning to slavery. Pain and death returned them to reality.

Please permit a personal illustration. We had a young son who was very "rambunctious" and "high-strung." He was given a tricycle for Christmas. In about two days, he had learned how to bank it at high speed so that he could ride it on two wheels only. He had also found the joys of riding in the street. We had a serious talk about confining our activities to the sidewalk. He agreed. I finished the lecture and started to enjoy the evening paper. This was interrupted by the screech of brakes and the blast of a horn.

I got up from my chair and looked out the window. In the street in front of our house was our son, looking up at a large truck that had been able to stop in time and had not run over him and his tricycle. A frightened father can spank about as hard as anyone and the boy's punishment was inflicted severely. A half hour later he was still in tears. At this point I noticed something in the paper I was reading, and called him over to see it.

"Son, do you see this boy?" I pointed to the picture in the paper of a child that had been taken to the hospital. The boy in the newspaper picture was in bad shape with several broken bones and a cracked head.

"What's the matter with him, Daddy?"

"He was riding his cycle in the street and he got hit by a truck."

There was a moment's silence while the significance of this sunk in. Then the concept came through that I had punished him because of his own best interests. In a sheepish way, he said, "I'm sorry, Daddy."

Fellowship was restored.

The Old Testament story parallels this. The snakes were a "gift" from God. The God of the Israelites knew that the temporary discomfort of the wilderness, followed by the promised land, was better for His children than years of slavery, death and extinction. Any man who could "see" the snake in that light, could also see and understand that the punishment was for his best interests. He lived.

It would seem that most of this was lost on Nicodemus. He didn't understand, and he didn't align himself with Jesus through the rest of the story. When Nicodemus was "put on the spot" in the end of the seventh chapter of John, he refused to be counted with those who are known as followers of Jesus. It would seem, though, that comprehension came on the day Jesus was crucified. As Nicodemus saw that body lifted on the cross and outlined against the sky, the words that he had heard that night three years before must have come back to him. "As Moses lifted the serpent in the wilderness, so must the Son of Man be lifted up."

Nicodemus had seen the power of Jesus in the cleansing of the temple. He knew that Jesus didn't have to be on that cross. He knew that, three years before, he had been told that this was the way the story would end. God was showing Nicodemus, as He shows us all, what we're like as a human race. Turned loose, we'll murder Jesus.

Nicodemus then did another courageous thing. He went with a fellow Jew named Joseph of Arimathea to the praetorium, the Roman governor's headquarters. Together they asked the governor for the dead body of Jesus. When Nicodemus did this he violated the rules of his religion. He made contact with a Gentile on the day of the Passover and was thereby made "unclean."

He went even further. The Old Testament Law had some things to say about touching a dead body. There were some very strict rules. When those two Jews took that body down off the cross they turned their backs on much that was traditionally sacred. <u>Traditions that made them righteous in their own eyes</u>.

It was Nicodemus' way of saying, "I'm sorry, Daddy."

You may call it what you will; an act of contrition, a demonstration of repentance, or an identification with Jesus. It matters little how it is named. It was the point at which Nicodemus <u>let go of his righteousness and opened himself</u> to something that <u>comes in from outside, from above.</u> It's the moment at which Nicodemus was "born again."

". . . So must the Son of Man be lifted up."
His pain and shame
I could no longer bear to see.
It was better then to break the law,
Than violate His love for me.

Three years before,
Foreshadowing His death and pain,
His words echoed in my mind
Now in my heart they will remain.

The Samaritan Woman

During the time of Jesus, the area loosely described as Palestine was divided ethnically into three parts. Hebrews lived in the southern part, Judea, and in the northern part, Galilee. In between them lay Samaria, an area filled with Samaritans, not Hebrews.

The division came about when the Assyrians conquered the territory during the reign of Shalmaneser or of his successor, Sargon the Second. In keeping with Assyrian policy, the Hebrew inhabitants were transported to Babylon, and other conquered peoples were moved from the Babylonian area into the center of Palestine. It was good politics. It let the Assyrians do as they pleased with conquered territories. Those who were displaced had no proprietary interest in the area in which they were forced to live. It wasn't their country and the Assyrians could exploit it as they pleased.

Those who had been imported into Palestine became known as Samaritans. They found the area very unfriendly and unhealthy. Thinking that they might have offended the local god, they petitioned Sargon II asking him to send someone back from Babylon who would instruct them in the ways of the God of the Hebrews. The request was granted; a Hebrew familiar with the Law was sent to Samaria. The Samaritans thereupon included the writings of Moses and Moses' God in with their other religions.

As the Hebrews reentered their land, they moved into the Judean or southern area first and then Galilee in the north. In due time they found themselves with a foreign people separating the two parts of their country, foreigners who had become acclimated and weren't about to go back to their original home. This situation was uncomfortable politically and militarily. Religiously it was intolerable. The Jews were passionately monotheistic and the mixture of their God and their Scripture into the polytheistic menage of the Samaritans was repulsive.

The hatred and the prejudice against Samaritans grew as the years went by until no Jew would walk through Samaritan territory. Human nature being what it is, the dislike was returned with interest, and in short order, the Samaritans had no dealings with the Hebrews.

This situation made the walk from Judea to Galilee a little complicated for the Jew. To avoid Samaritans a Jew would walk east from Jerusalem to Jericho. At Jericho he would cross the Jordan River and walk north on the east bank until he was parallel with Galilee. Then he would cross the river into Hebrew territory.

This is the point of the story of Jesus about "The Good Samaritan." The Jew in the story is on the road to Jericho when he falls among thieves and is robbed and beaten. He was on the road to Jericho to keep from meeting Samaritans. Jesus makes the hero of the story, who rescues the Jew, a "good Samaritan." In its own day, the story carried a sting.

In the fourth chapter of John we read that Jesus, on His way north from Judea to Galilee "had to pass through Samaria." To have done otherwise would have been to acquiesce to the prejudice of His own people and His own time. This He would not do.

The walk north was long, hot and dusty. During the heat of the middle of one day, He and His disciples came to the well outside the Samaritan city of Sychar. Jesus sat on the edge of the well, while His disciples went into town to purchase food. They went in a group probably for mutual protection. It was not a friendly environment. By leaving Jesus outside of the town, at the well, they may have thought that they were protecting Him from contaminating influences.

After they had left, a Samaritan woman approached the well with her water jar to draw water. This was an indication of a problem.

The women of the city went to the well in the cool of the morning, or the cool of the evening. No one would come alone in the heat of the day unless there was a social or personal problem.

Jesus, obviously a Jew, spoke first. This was unusual enough, but even more startling was the fact that He asked for a favor, "Give Me a drink."

The Samaritan woman decided that she must be talking to a very thirsty Jew. One so thirsty that He would ask a favor of a Samaritan woman and a "shady lady" to boot. It looked to her like a situation that could be exploited. She decided to jab Him a little.

"How come, You, a Jew, asks a favor of a Samaritan woman?"

"If you knew the gift that comes from God and who it is that is asking you for a drink, you would ask Him for living water."

In all probability they were talking in a language called Koine Dialektos. It was Greek in origin and a language common to both Jews and Samaritans. It is capable of great subtlety. There are several words for "living" and in some measure they are used interchangeably, but generally speaking, "bios," where we get the word "biology," was used for common life. The word "zoe" is used for spiritual life. In later Christian literature it is used for "life in the Holy Spirit." It is this word that Jesus used when He said "living" water.

The significance was lost on her. She still wanted to "needle." "You don't have anything with which to draw water, and this well is deep. Where do You get living water? Are You greater than our father Jacob, who gave us this well?"

Within the context in which it was spoken it was insulting. The Jew hated the thought of a common ancestry with the Samaritan and wouldn't admit it for a second. Even worse, the Jew believed that the well had been given to the Hebrew nation. The Samaritans had no right to it. She thought that Jesus was thirsty enough to swallow the insult.

He ignored it. "Whoever drinks this water will be thirsty for it again, but whoever drinks the water that I give shall never thirst again. And this water will become a spring within himself, bubbling up to eternal life."

He had her undivided attention and they switched roles. "Sir, give me this water that I will not get thirsty and I won't have to come here to draw."

That is one of the most pathetic sentences in literature. The significance of "zoe" was still lost on her. She was still thinking "bios," but the terrible loneliness of an ostracized life shows through her request. There is no greater social pain than that caused by the rejection of one's peers. If she came to draw water in the morning or the evening the other women would insult her. If she came in the middle of the day, she was advertising the fact that their insults "got to her." She lost either way. It was coming through to her that this strange young Jew could do something to alleviate her situation. The one petitioned had become the petitioner.

Jesus said, "Go get your husband and bring him here also."

The man with whom she was living was not a man in whom she could have any pride. In addition, the Law of Moses, in some areas, applied to Samaritan as well as to Jew. A woman married only once. She was a legal wife of her first husband until he died.

"Sir, I have no husband."

Jesus smiled, "Yes, I know. This is number five, and you're right when you say he's not your husband."

There was a stunned silence. The shoe was completely on the other foot now. "Sir, I perceive that You are a prophet. You Jews say that Jerusalem is the place where we have to go to worship. We say here in Samaria that it is on this mountain that men ought to worship. Who is right?"

The psychology of this conversation is perfect at this point. Any time moral standards are unfavorably applied, the next question has to do with comparative religion. Show us that we are wrong, or tell us that we are wrong, and we'll challenge the basis of judgment every time. I know of no culture anywhere in the world that has been even remotely touched by the Judaeo-Christian ethic where a woman who had lived with five different men would consider her moral life a smashing success. Jesus had touched a raw spot. She put up the best possible defense, the grey area of eclectic religion and its accompanying indecisive morality.

The beauty of the answer Jesus gives her is that it makes her question superfluous. "Neither on this mountain nor in Jerusalem." Notice that He didn't say "either," He said "neither." This remark, and the subsequent conversation, ends forever the concept of a "place of worship" for those who take the words of Jesus seriously.

"You Samaritans do not know what you worship. Up until now, salvation has been through the Jews, for God has revealed Himself through them. But the hour is coming and is here now when those who worship the Father must worship Him in Spirit and in truth, for God seeks such to worship Him."

With this, Jesus is back to His argument with the Jewish authorities. "Destroy this temple and in three days I will raise it up." The temple of His body. He is opening in more detail to the Samaritan woman the possibility of direct communication with God apart from "sacred" buildings, "sacred" days or religious devices. His point is that God is Spirit and He can reach us through that portion of His Spirit, or His nature that He will put within us if we let Him.

The Samaritan woman was out of her depth and she knew it. She had one more card to play. The Messianic hope, the concept of the coming world ruler that was the hope of the Jew had been inappropriately applied to the Samaritans by the Samaritans. She needled once more.

"All I know is that when the Christ comes, He'll explain all this."

Jesus looked at her and smiled. She spoke more truth than she knew, for there was to be a universal quality about the coming Messiah. "It is the Christ to whom you are speaking."

This tells us something more about the woman; for where people are indecisive, Jesus is evasive. He spoke bluntly to those who had rejected the truth. Also He spoke frankly and openly to those who were volitionally committed to the truth, if and when they could find it. A good guess would be that this woman had already made up her mind that if and when God sent His prophet, the one she had been told about, she'd believe in Him. The writer of the Gospel points to one minor fact that somewhat substantiates this. She ran back to Sychar without her water pot.

In that culture and at that time among peo-ple of limited means, a properly "sweating" water pot that kept the water cool was not an inexpensive item. Had she been anything but overwhelmed, she would not have left hers at the well. But she left it, and in that heat she ran back to Sychar.

"I have found Him. He told me all about myself. He knew. Could this be the Christ? Come and see . . . come and see . . ."

Who is this Man
Who looks at me
And sees what shame would hide?
And Living Water—
Can there be
An Eternal Spring inside?

Perhaps He is the Christ

But why should He care to set me free,
Knowing what He knows of me?

The Cripple

It is possible to know something about a man by the friends that he makes and by watching how he makes them. The same can be said concerning a man's enemies.

We have been looking at people to whom Jesus has been attractive. Now we'll look at some who took a different point of view concerning Him. Most of His opposition came from the conservative branch of the ruling body of the Hebrew Nation. The governing council was called the Sanhedrin and the conservative party within it was called the Pharisaical party, or the party of the Pharisees.

Because of their connection with the death of Jesus, the term Pharisee has taken on a connotation that it did not have in its own day. As we shall see as we go, many of the enemies of Jesus were numbered among the "best" people. The Pharisees were patriotic, they really loved their land and their heritage, and more than one of them died for it. They worshiped the Law and the prophets and had them thoroughly memorized. They hired students of "The Law and the Traditions" to accompany them and to instruct them so that they did not violate even the most minor Tradition. (These men who studied these matters professionally are called "lawyers" in the New Testament story.)

As community leaders, as rulers of the temple, they commanded the respect, even the awe, of the common people. They brooked no challenge to their authority, religious or temporal, and they hated Rome and the Roman occupation. They soon learned to hate Jesus.

In the fifth chapter of John, Jesus enters, on the Sabbath day, what was in that culture a "hospital." It was five "porches," or level areas surrounding a pool of water. The place was called Bethesda. There was a Jewish superstition that an angel would move the water from time to time and the first sick or crippled person who immersed himself into the pool after the water was "troubled" would be cured. This information was made part of the text by some third century scribe who wanted to explain the subsequent conversation to those who would have no way of knowing about the superstition. However the fourth verse of the fifth chapter is not part of the original document.

As the story begins, Jesus walks among the sick and crippled and picks out a man who has been there for thirty-eight years. Jesus asks him a question. "Do you want to be healed?"

This would seem strange to some observers but it shows an insight into the psychology of illness. A man learns to be sick, he learns to be dependent, and the day can come when the idea of reentering the competitive world of sweat, toil and responsibility is not appealing. It is easier to stay sick and let someone wait on you.

Such was not the case with this man. He seems to be ashamed of the length of his stay, and his answer shows his concern. "Sir, there is no one who will wait here with me and when the water is 'troubled,' someone else always gets in ahead of me."

Jesus said, "Get up, wrap up your bed and walk out of here."

This short sentence has in it the three characteristics of the relationship between Jesus and some of those whom He healed. The crippled man was told to do what he could not do, get up. If he hadn't tried, he'd still be there. It has deep theological significance. Faith and obedience cannot be separated.

Second, he had to burn his bridges behind him. If he tried to do as he was told and partially succeeded, he could lose his place on the porch. After thirty-eight years of lying there, he would be pretty close to the water. If he summoned enough strength to move away a little, but was not healed, his place in line was gone.

Third, he was told to put his newly given strength to work. He was to carry his bed: walk and carry. He did as he was told and the strength was supplied.

Any good Jew, so healed, would head for the temple to offer praise and thanksgiving. He proceeded to do so, but the problem was that Jesus had healed him on the Sabbath. The word of the prophet Jeremiah is very clear. "Take heed to yourself and bear no burden on the Sabbath day."

His path was crossed by a group of Pharisees. They were jealous for the traditions and they enforced them. Because of their financial power and moral influence within the community they were able to do just that. "You are breaking the Law. You cannot carry your bed on the Sabbath."

The man's answer is revealing. He knew the law, but in his mind if someone could heal him after thirty-eight years of illness, that someone could tell him to break the law. "The man who healed me said, 'take up your bed and walk.' "

Their response is an example of the inflexibility of the religiously indoctrinated mind. "Who is this man who told you to take up your bed and walk?"

Let's put this in perspective. Supposing a man has been in a hospital for years. A stranger walks in, picks him out from among the others in the ward, cures the man and tells him to go home.

The cured man gets dressed, runs out of the hospital, hails a cab and goes home. His wife meets him at the door and he says, "Honey, a man came into the hospital and cured me. I'm not sick anymore. I took a taxi home."

If, in response to this, she should ask him in an angry tone, "Why did you come home in a taxi?" she would show that their relationship was not a warm one.

In our story, a man has been sick for thirty-eight years. Now he's well, he's walking, and he's going to the temple to give thanks. The Pharisees don't ask, "Who healed you?" nor do they say, "That's wonderful news," instead they bristle and ask, "Who is the man who told you to carry your bed?"

The man healed couldn't answer. The implication of the text is that Jesus left the scene so rapidly that the cripple couldn't even express his appreciation. "I don't know who it was."

This brings us to a characteristic of Jesus that bothered the Pharisees. It bothers us too. Why didn't Jesus stay in the center of the hospital until everyone was cured? There would have been great rejoicing and overwhelming evidence on behalf of His power. Why cure just one man? Why tell the cured man to violate the Law?

There is something "cross-grained" about Jesus. He is constantly going upstream. There

are three ways in which this characteristic net-
tles us. First, Jesus did not seem to be interested
in what went on in this world unless it influenced what was to happen in the next. If
healing the sick interfered with the presenta-
tion of the coming kingdom of God, He didn't
heal. If healing the sick would advance the
knowledge of the kingdom of God, He healed.
He would not treat this world nor life in this
world as an end in itself (i.e., ". . . he who hates
his life in this world shall keep it unto life eternal . . ."). The Jewish rulers were looking for
a kingdom of God in the "here and now," a
kingdom that gave them worldly leverage. To
them the ability of Jesus to influence people
was frightening, for He constantly talked to the
common people about a world that was really
important, one that they could not yet see. To
the Pharisees, as to most of us, the world that
can be seen is important enough.

Second, Jesus was never interested in giving overwhelming evidence to the uncommit-
ted concerning Himself and His claims. The
evidence He presented was enough to make
His claims possible, but the volitional aspect
was never removed by a naked display of un-
limited power. The individual's integrity was
never violated. When Jesus was through talking and demonstrating, the decision to accept
or reject what He had said still rested on the

shoulders of the listener. Jesus wanted only those who wanted Him, not those who by overpowering evidence were forced to believe in something that was contrary to their own basic desires.

The third thing, and the most aggravating of all, is that He never seemed to work in any way that gave approval to that which man thought to be "right." He never did anything to praise human righteousness, particularly when that righteousness was "credited" to God. What we mean by this will be spelled out subsequently in an argument between Jesus and the Pharisees.

He seemed to have deliberately picked the Sabbath for the healing. If he had chosen any other day, there would not have been a confrontation with the religious leaders. When the desired confrontation did not occur because the healed man didn't know the name of Jesus, Jesus went to the temple to find him and identified Himself. By so doing He gave the healed man the information to give to the Pharisees. This action made the confrontation possible.

Notice that He identified Himself to the man in a way that has significance in terms of the next world. He said, "Now that you are a well man, stop practicing your sinful ways or something worse will happen to you." It is possible that the something worse had to do with eternity. In terms of this world, thirty-eight years of illness would seem to be about as bad as things can get.

It might do to say in passing that there is an uneven relationship between sin and illness in the book of John as there is in everyday life. Not all sin results in immediate illness. Not all illness is the result of immediate sin. There are times when the two come together. "Overindulgence" can bring a nasty "hangover" the following day, and adultery can result in syphilis. Both drunkenness and sexual promiscuity are sins under the Mosaic covenant. It is safe to say that whether or not the man had a virulent sexual disease, he did have something which was the physical result of that which he believed to be morally wrong. The implication is that the physical suffering because of physical sin, bad as it was, would be surpassed by spiritual suffering because of spiritual sin.

When the man knew that it was Jesus who had cured him, he went to the temple rulers and did a little informing. He let them know it was Jesus who had told him to carry his bed. There are a couple of possible motivations for his actions. He might have wanted to take the "monkey" off his own back. He had broken the Law in obedience to Jesus, so he passed the "buck." If this was the motivation, informing was a most ungrateful act. It would seem better to assume that he knew Jesus wanted the confrontation. If there was no confrontation desired, the day after the Sabbath would have done just as well as far as the healing was concerned. It would also be fair to assume that the cured man could feel that anyone who could order the disease out of another man's body, could take care of himself with the Pharisees. If Jesus wanted a confrontation with the rulers of the temple, it was all right with the man who had been crippled.

The confrontation soon took place. Pharisaical punishment for violation of the Law was swift, sure and sometimes cruel. When they accused Jesus of violating the Sabbath, His comment was cryptic. "My Father works and I work too." This doesn't mean too much to us, but to a group of Jewish theologians the implication was clear enough. What Jesus is saying is that the Sabbath does not change the nature nor the work of God. The sun still shines, the rain falls, the wind blows, life goes on, seven full days a week. God doesn't cease to be God on the Sabbath. He continues to sustain the universe. If Jesus was claiming a common nature with the Father and Jesus healed the sick during the first six days of the week, then He would have to heal on the seventh also.

This threw fuel on the fire. They accused

Him angrily of making Himself equal with God. His answer to this charge is subtle and deep.

"The works that I do are not Mine, the Father is doing them through Me."

How do we judge a man? Many ways perhaps, but the most objective way is to look at what he says and how he says it, and then look at what he does and how he does it. We reveal to the outside world our nature by the history of our words and our actions.

If we walk into a bank and ask the banker to cash our check, there may be several things that influence him as he talks to us. He may look at our clothes, our manner of speech, our self-confidence, etc., but experience has taught him not to take these things too seriously. The "proper approach" is too easily imitated by a good "con artist." If the banker is considering whether or not to cash our check he is really interested in whether or not we have done and said certain things in the past few years. He will judge us on the basis of our past word and our past actions.

This is the argument that Jesus proposes to His enemies in the fifth, sixth, seventh and eighth chapters of John. He says, ". . . The words that I speak are not Mine, the Father gave them to Me. The works that I do are not Mine, the Father is doing them through Me . . .

Judge with true judgment . . . Judge Me by what the Father has given Me to say . . . and by the works given to Me by the Father . . ."

This concept enables Him to make a couple of points. One of them is this. "As you honor the Son so you honor the Father. If you do not honor the Son you do not honor the Father who sent Him." Why?

We all have a picture of God or of a non-god in our minds. We made it up for ourselves, and it is the product of heredity and early environment. We all serve this concept one way or another. It may be our concept of "the good," or we may think we live in keeping with the principles of "mother" nature, or "basic" morality, or lust, or appetite, or pride. Something is driving us or keeping us from being driven. Jesus is telling the Pharisees, and down through the centuries he's telling us, that the picture of God that is accurate is the picture generated by the words and acts of Jesus. Any concept of God that does not match the image so created is a concept that will not stand up in the day of Judgment.

". . . Even those who are in the tombs will hear the voice of the Son of Man and come forth . . . to the resurrection of life . . . or the resurrection of judgment . . ."

The idea that they, the Pharisees (or we) should look at a poverty-stricken, unschooled, dust-covered Galilean peasant and equate that with the Almighty is repugnant. Jesus puts His finger on the reason.

". . . You study your Scripture unceasingly because you think that in Scripture there is life eternal, but you do not come to Me that you might receive life, because I do not receive glory from men . . . How can you believe, you who receive glory from each other? . . ."

Jesus is accusing them (and us) of playing a game, "I'll treat you as though you were a 'nice guy' and you treat me as though I'm a 'nice guy' and we'll neither one of us have to face the fact that we're a couple of genuine stinkers." Jesus wouldn't play the game.

". . . I have come in the Father's name and you will not accept Me. When someone else comes in his own name, you'll accept him . . ." If a man comes in his own name (a Hebrewism meaning in his own interests) there is a handle on him. If he doesn't butter your bread, you don't have to butter his. There was no way for the Pharisees to play "tit-for-tat" with a man who wanted to give all the glory to the Father. Jesus wanted no praise for Himself, therefore He didn't have to give any praise to others and dialogue with Him boiled down to disgusting reality.

This is the way Jesus cornered the "rich young ruler" in the Gospel of Luke. He asked the young man, "Why do you call me good?

There is none good but God." Jesus refuses to see human "good" as good or human "morality" as moral, "there is none good but God." He claims goodness for Himself, real goodness because He is able to say, ". . . I can do nothing on My own . . . I seek not My own will, but the will of Him who sent Me . . ."

In order to explain something of the motivation of Jesus, we'll get ahead of our story a little. He is preparing the Pharisee and the common man to face the fact that God is approached successfully when man asks for mercy and not justice. He prepares man for the need for mercy by undermining man's concept of self-righteousness. "There is none good but God." When His words are understood, they sting. This goes for the Pharisee of two thousand years ago and for the Christian of today. There is still none good but God.

Let's recap our thinking by looking at one more phrase by the writer of the Gospel. ". . . This is why the Jews (remember, that's a religious term) sought to kill Him. He broke the Sabbath and . . . made Himself the equal of God . . ."

The Sabbath is a useful command to the self-righteous. It can be kept so publicly. You notice the Pharisees didn't brag about their righteousness in terms of the seventh commandment, "Thou shalt not commit adultery," and Jesus chided them about this elsewhere,

". . . you go to the homes of widows and pretend to make very long prayers . . ." The Pharisees picked the commandment that didn't interfere with what they really wanted to do, the commandment to keep the Sabbath, and then considered themselves righteous because they obeyed it.

Human nature hasn't changed. Ask a man about his moral life and he'll give you a list of his virtues in a negative way. He didn't want to beat his wife anyway.

Because the commandment of God to keep the Sabbath was being used by men as an excuse to consider themselves moral, Jesus refused to be bound by the Sabbath. There is no faster way to stir up a storm in a religious environment than to refuse its shibboleths.

The second half of our quotation from John is even more to the point. ". . . he made Himself equal with God . . ." As we read about God in almost all religions we are told that He is "all powerful," He is omnipotent, He is everlasting. These characteristics are easy for the religious to accept. A man can bow to such a being with his pride intact. Jesus reveals a part of the nature of God that is not revealed by any other religion up until His time, and not revealed by any other religion since unless it is copying Him. Jesus showed that a characteristic of God is humility. How then can we bow to Him with our pride intact?

The trouble with humility is that it comes through humiliation. The humiliation of the Godhead is the incarnation of Jesus. He became man and dwelt among us. Many a Jew could accept this. There were plenty of students of the Old Testament who expected something like the incarnation, but their picture was one that left human pride intact. They were looking for a glorious, all powerful leader to whom the whole world would have to bow. A leader that would point out to the world the way to increase the "goodness" and "righteousness" which man has in his own nature. A leader who would build on what is already here.

Instead, God showed Himself in Jesus by poverty, humiliation, degradation and death. He arranged this demonstration in such a way that the righteousness of man could be shown for what it is. It was those who most loudly proclaimed their goodness and their faithfulness to God and to the "right" who laid the plans for the murder of the only man whoever perfectly pictured the nature of the Father.

To rise and walk
After a life of waiting
For a miracle.

To rise and walk
After a life of hoping
For a chance.

He came and said
"Rise up and walk.
Go home. Be on your way."
It was the miracle of His Voice
The waters did not move that day.

The Man Born Blind

The antagonism between the temple leaders and Jesus became overt after the healing of the cripple. To the consternation of the Pharisees, He pressed His claims publicly.

The "Feast of the Tabernacles" referred to in the seventh chapter was an annual custom ordered by the Old Testament and strictly adhered to by the religious among the Hebrews. It was a time when the exodus from Egypt into the wilderness was celebrated. Jews from every stratum of society went to Jerusalem for the feast and "camped out." Each family built its own "booth" or in our language, pitched its own tent, and lived for one week each year as their forefathers had lived during the forty years between Egypt and the promised land.

The celebration was climaxed by "the drawing of the water." The priests took one of the golden vessels from the temple and went to the pool of Siloam and filled it. This was followed by a stately procession back to the temple where the water was poured out on the ground. It was done in memory of the provision God had made for His people in the wilderness. It was heavy with significance. Among other things, it was a way of saying thanks for the rain that had made the preceding harvest possible.

To the spiritual it had still deeper significance. One of the prophets had promised that some day the Jews would draw water from the "Wells of Salvation." The pouring of the water was a request to God to send His Spirit upon Israel as He had in days of old. When the water was poured out, there was a moment's silence while those assembled waited to see if this was the year in which God would answer.

On this occasion the moment of silence was broken by the voice of Jesus. It could be heard by many in the assembled multitude as He cried out, "If anyone is thirsty let him come to Me and drink and as the Scriptures have prophesied, out of his innermost being will flow rivers of water that lives."

To understand the enormity of this offense, we must put ourselves in the position of the high priest. To him, the man, the act, and the voice were offensive. Jesus was Galilean. That meant that his accent was Galilean also. Let's put the scene in modern dress.

Supposing His Holiness the Pope came from Rome and said mass in Saint Patrick's Cathedral in New York City. If, while His Holiness paused for a moment in the celebration of the mass, a voice from the back of the room, a voice, mind you, with a strong Brooklyn accent called out, "Hey, fellows, if you want a real communion, come back here and I'll serve you." Pandemonium would reign supreme.

What Jesus said was blasphemous to those who did not believe that He was the Christ, and there can be little doubt that the feast was ruined for the religious leaders. That's not all. The offense was repeated.

At the close of the celebration (the Jewish day began at sunset) lamps were prepared and placed around the temple. When darkness came, and the feast was officially over, the lamps were lighted as simultaneously as possible. At this moment, a great shout went up from the crowd in honor of the pillar of fire that had lighted the way for the Israelites of Old. In the moment of darkness, just before the lamps were lighted, this Galilean accent was heard again. To the horror of the temple authorities, Jesus cried out:

"If any man follows Me, he will not walk in darkness. He will have the light of spiritual Life."

The Pharisees didn't take this lying down. These incidents were surrounded by face-to-face confrontations and bitter argument. The Pharisees grew so bitter in fact that they finally accused Jesus of being possessed by a demon.

In the middle of the temple courtyard, surrounded by the crowds, Jesus "took them on." "I am not possessed by a demon. I upset you

because I honor My Father. In return you dis-
honor Me. You do this because unlike you, I
do not seek My own glory. There is One who
will take care of that for Me. He will be your
judge. His judgment on you for dishonoring
Me will be spiritual death. Please listen to Me.
If any one of you will believe what I say and
follow what I say, you will be delivered from
death."

They answered with hatred that was inten-
sifying. "Now we have proof that you're possessed by a demon. Our Father Abraham died,
all the prophets died, and yet You have the
audacity to say, 'If anyone of you will believe
what I say and follow what I say, you will be
delivered from death.' Are you greater than
Abraham, our father, who died? Are you
greater than all the prophets who died? Who
do you think you are?"

Jesus answered, "What I think of myself is
not the point. I don't glorify Myself as you glorify yourselves. My Father will glorify Me in
His own good time. You say that My Father is
your God and you are liars. I know that you
don't know Him. I know Him. If you knew
Him you would honor Him by honoring Me.
If I said, 'I don't know Him,' then I would be
a liar like the rest of you. You do the will of
your father the devil, he was a liar from the
beginning. You do not do God's will, and you
do not keep His word. I do His will and keep

His word. Even Abraham, whom you say is your father, rejoiced over the fact that he was to see My day. He has seen it and he is glad."

The Jews said to him, "You're insane. You're not yet fifty years old. When did you see Abraham?"

Jesus said, "Listen to Me carefully. Before Abraham was, I am."

The verb "I am" was the name of God used by God in His conversation with Moses at the burning bush. It was a flat claim on the part of Jesus to the nature of Deity. The Jews had two choices. They could worship Him, or accuse Him of blasphemy. The penalty for blasphemy was painful. A man got himself stoned to death. The Jews bent over in the temple courtyard and started picking up the "bricks" with which it was paved. Jesus knew how and when He was to die. It wasn't to be by stoning and the time was not yet. Because it was the Sabbath the courtyard was full of people and He slipped into the crowd and out of the temple. Some of His disciples managed to escape with Him.

As they left by one of the side gates, they passed a beggar who had seated himself in that one spot for years, begging his daily bread. It was a pathetic sight. The disciples were "this world" minded and they believed that sight was an inalienable right. If this man was born blind, somebody had made a mistake.

"Teacher," they asked Jesus, "who sinned? This man or his parents? He was born blind."

Jesus answered, "Neither this man nor his parents." Jesus accepted the Mosaic concept that because sin entered the world, and because man lives out of fellowship with his Creator, there is suffering, sickness and death, but He also followed the book of Job, and refused to make a one-to-one correlation. That is, one particular sin does not always end in one particular suffering, and one particular piece of suffering does not necessarily come as the result of one particular sin. As Job teaches, the "righteous" suffer too.

Jesus continued. "This man was born blind because God wanted to use his blindness to show that He is working. He is working through Me; while I'm in the world I'm the light of the world, and the ending of this man's blindness is a 'sign,' a manifestation of the power of God."

As Jesus spoke, He spat on the ground and made clay in the dust. This clay was placed on the man's eyelids. There may have been a good reason for this. C. S. Lewis argues persuasively that the public works of Jesus fit in the patterns of nature as we know them. The Scriptures stated that "He remembers how we are made; we are made of dust."

Whether one accepts the concept of creation as it is in the book of Genesis, or whether one goes along with contemporary theories concerning the origin of life, the place of origin is still the same. It's mud. If the man had no eyes, Jesus made him new ones from the same substance that was used in creation (or evolution).

After He had applied the mud, He said: "Go to the pool of Siloam (a word which means 'sent') and wash."

Biblical expositors for years have tried to make something out of the word "siloam," trying to show that it had some significance in the healing. It would seem that the reason Jesus sent him there was simple and obvious. When Jesus healed the cripple, He told him to carry his bed which was a violation of the Sabbath. When He gave this man sight He placed the same stigma on him. There were laws concerning how far a man might walk on the Sabbath day. A "Sabbath's day's journey" wasn't very far. It was farther from the temple to the Pool than the Law permitted a man to walk.* The beggar had his choice. He could keep the Sabbath and stay blind, or he could violate the

---

* This is unproven, but not unsubstantiated. Acts 1:12 gives a Sabbath day's journey as Mt. Olivet to the temple's East gate, the East gate seems to have been the Jewish point of reckoning. That distance is about twenty-two hundred feet. From the East gate to the pool is more than that, and from the East gate to the pool and back to the temple could have been more than an English mile.

Sabbath at the command of Jesus and receive his sight. It is hard to think of a way Jesus could have made the healing more infuriating to the Pharisees.

The man chose to obey Jesus. He went and washed and walked back to the temple seeing. The face of a man born blind, or born without eyes, is apt to be vacuous. When sight was given, there was a decided change in expression. His friends weren't sure they knew him. They began to look at him curiously and nudge one another.

"Is that the man born blind?"

He put their doubts to rest. "I am the man born blind, the one who used to beg at the gate."

A matter of this moment had to be taken before the council. The man born blind had not only been healed on the Sabbath, he'd walked too far. They took him to the Pharisees.

Let's put some things in here that show the courage of this man. He was a poverty-stricken beggar. The Pharisees were rich. They had the community by the throat. They controlled it politically, socially, economically and religiously. A man could incur their wrath and starve to death, both the man and his family.

The Pharisees were seated in their places in the council and they looked down on this beggar in every way there is to look down. They questioned him. "How did you receive your sight?"

"A man named Jesus anointed my eyes with clay and told me to walk down to the pool of Siloam and wash. I did, and when I washed off the clay, I could see."

Some of the Pharisees said: "This man Jesus is not from God. If He were, He wouldn't have told you to break the Sabbath by walking to the pool."

Once again the intransigence of the religiously indoctrinated mind shows through. The fact that a man who had been born blind had now received his sight wasn't important. What was important was that the rule of the true religion given by God hadn't been obeyed. The rule, that is, that they used to convince themselves that they were "godly."

There was an argument within the council. One can easily suspect that it came from Nicodemus. "How can a man who lives apart from God give a man born blind his sight?"

This was a good question. It might be wise to drop the matter, but one thing had to be determined first. Had this man been pulled out from under their authority by the receiving of his sight? Was Jesus pulling people away from the temple and to Himself? The next question was crucial as to whether or not the matter would be pursued further.

"What do you say of this man, now that you have received your sight?" Notice they didn't say, Now that He has given you your sight. They gave the man born blind a chance to "welch" a little.

He wouldn't buy it. "This man is a prophet."

From the Pharisee's point of view, he just "blew it." The authority of a prophet of God exceeded the authority of the temple leadership. The man had paid Jesus the highest praise he dared pay. For the moment, the man knew nothing higher than a prophet. His answer meant that he recognized religious authority apart from the temple, and he attributed that authority to God. From the Pharisees' point of view, he had to be squelched. Maybe they could undermine the man's story by undermining his premise. Could he prove he'd been born blind?

They sent for his parents. His father and mother came with fear and trembling. It was like being invited to the Spanish Inquisition. The spokesman for the council addressed them.

"Is this man your son? Is he the one you allege was born blind?" He paused for a moment before he went on. "How does it happen that now he can see?"

The implication was clear. They had three ways out. They could claim he was not their son, or that he was not born blind. The third was a little harder, but they could, if they wanted to do so, come up with a story about how he had received his sight in the temple. Any one of the three answers would have been satisfactory to the Pharisees, and the parents could have departed in peace.

They showed a little courage. They didn't lie about what they knew, but they didn't volunteer any information either. In all probability they had heard that it was Jesus who had healed their son. They didn't want to say so, and it is hard to blame them. The council had ruled that anyone admitting that Jesus was the Christ was automatically excluded from the synagogue. That could mean religious death, social ostracism, economic ruin, and in some cases, physical torture.

It is enough that they had the courage to answer as they did. How their son received his sight was "hearsay" and they were not legally bound to repeat it. They stuck to the truth in the area where they had firsthand knowledge.

"This is our son. He was born blind. If you want to know how he received his sight, please ask him, sir. He is over twenty-one. Let him speak for himself."

The Pharisees had lost another round. They turned again to the man born blind. "Give the praise for this to God. We know that Jesus is a sinner."

"Whether or not Jesus is a sinner is something I wouldn't know about. One thing I do know. I was born blind and now I can see." If we may be permitted a rough word, that answer took a lot of guts.

The council had lost still another round. They resorted to an old trick, familiar to all lawyers. Get a man to repeat a story enough times, and from different perspectives, and sooner or later, he'll contradict himself on some minor point.

"What did Jesus do to you? How did He open your eyes?"

The witness wouldn't fall for it. He answered with a question that impugned their motives. "We went over this once. How come you want to hear it again? Do you also want to become His disciples?"

He might as well have stuck a knife in them. The text says that they "reviled" him. That's a gentle translation. Furthermore the Greek verb is conjugated in the third person plural. That means that the spokesman was drowned out in a roar of abuse delivered by the whole council. When the storm had subsided, the spokesman tried again.

"You are a disciple of Jesus? We are disciples of Moses. Now we know that God spoke to Moses, but we don't even know where this Jesus came from."

The witness was not intimidated. "We

know that God has little communication with men who are living in sin. We know that God listens to those who are trying to please Him. This Jesus is so close to God that He can open the eyes of a man born blind. This has never before happened in the history of Israel. This man is close enough to God to do it. You are supposed to know what is going on around here in terms of the working of God, and you're so far behind you don't even know where this man comes from. This is a marvel."

That hit home. "You would teach us, when you were born in utter sin!"

The significance of "utter sin" is that they were taking an unscriptural view of illness. They were implying that if this man were born blind, there was something sinful about his birth. In other words, he was a bastard or God would have let him be born with sight.

The Chinese have a saying, "He who strikes the first blow has lost the argument." That's true and the text says that "they cast him out." The word for "cast" is *ekballō*. Perhaps you can recognize "ball." They gave him the old "heave ho."

Word was passed to Jesus that the man born blind had been thrown out of the temple. Jesus went looking for him. He knew that for the man born blind, this would be a dark hour. The battle had been won, but the war lost. He had been a good Jew, and the temple was his link to the Almighty. This door was now closed to him and he had closed it on himself by testifying to the power of Jesus. His livelihood was gone. He was no longer blind and couldn't beg, but normal avenues of income are not open to men who have been marked "pariah" by their culture. Even his parents might have to run the gauntlet if they tried to help him in any way.

He was sitting in the dusty street, his back to a shady wall, gently rubbing his bruises when he became conscious of a man standing beside him. He had never seen Jesus. When they had first met he had been blind.

Jesus spoke first. "Do you believe in the Son of Man?"

He hadn't seen Jesus but he'd know that voice anywhere. It was the One that had told him to go wash in the pool of Siloam. Also he, like Nathanael, knew the meaning of the "Son of Man." It was Messianic. Suddenly there was hope in his heart.

"Who is the Son of Man? Tell me, sir, please, so I can believe in Him."

"Now you can see Him, and it is He who speaks to you."

The man fell at the feet of Jesus and worshiped, tears of joy streaming down his face.

Who needs a temple?

Why do you question
About my eyes?
A gift of sight
Can't be explained.
Is that why you're angry?
Or is your outcry one of fear?
Are you afraid to see His light?
And find your sight's a gift as well?

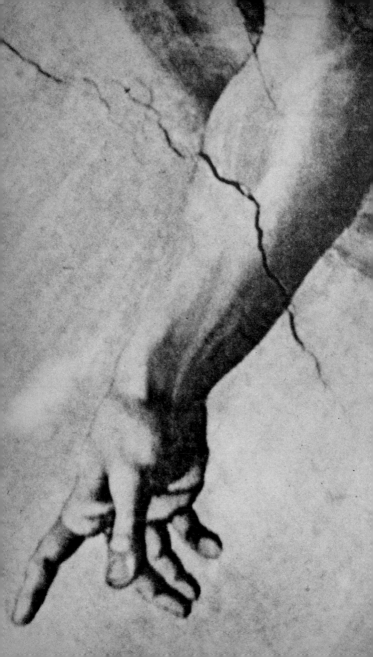

Lazarus

This picture has to do with a man named Lazarus. His testimony contrasts sharply with the testimony of Pontius Pilate in our following chapter. Pilate's judgment may be the most objective in the Gospel. Contrarily, this story is possibly the most subjective. It is also very beautiful. It describes the raising of Lazarus from the dead by the word of Jesus.

There are two factors that tend to give even this subjective story some sense of objectivity. The first factor is the silence of the writer concerning the experience of Lazarus while he was in the grave. If the story were faked, the faker would have a golden opportunity to give or to make up startling revelations concerning the hereafter, and attribute these revelations to Lazarus. We look in the text in vain for any such expected thing. There is a poem that deals with this insight. (I cannot find the author's name.) The last four lines go something like this:

> Behold a man raised up by Christ
> The rest remaineth unrevealed;
> He told it not; or something seal'd
> The lips of that Evangelist.

If the story of Lazarus is a fake, the liar passed up a golden opportunity to impress us.

The second indication of objectivity is the psychology of the conversation and the order of events. The story is not very flattering to the participants. If it were made up "after the fact" and neatly composed, the friends of Jesus could have been put in a much more favorable light.

Jesus was east of the Jordan River enjoying the comparative safety of that area, far from his enemies in the temple, when news reached Him from Bethany. Bethany was a small town very close to Jerusalem and in it was the home of three friends of Jesus: Lazarus and his sisters, Mary and Martha. It was Mary who, in a famous Gospel story, washed the feet of Jesus with perfume and tears and then wiped His feet with her hair. She sent word to Jesus concerning her brother Lazarus, "Lord, he whom You love is ill."

The text states that when Jesus received this news, because He loved the three of them, He stayed where He was. Here again is the annoying habit of Jesus. He refuses to see things in terms of the here and now. If any of this Gospel can be believed, the illness could have been ended short of death by Jesus, but He refused to meet the crisis. To have done so would have been to add simply one more healing to the many that had already transpired. Jesus waited until Lazarus died and then took action. This gave Him an opportunity to witness concerning Himself and the life to come on an altogether different plane. It also meant that Lazarus had to experience death, and that the two sisters had to endure the pain of a separation that they believed would be permanent.

Such separations are bad enough in any culture, but in that day and time, unmarried sisters were dependent upon their brothers in every aspect of life. In that household, the death of Lazarus was unmitigated tragedy. Jesus stayed away and let it happen. As always with Him, temporal sorrow is insignificant in comparison with the knowledge of spiritual reality.

When He was sure that Lazarus was dead, He said to His disciples, "Let us go back to Judea."

The disciples protested, "Teacher, the temple leaders were trying to stone You to death just a few days ago, why go back there?"

Jesus answered, "There are twelve hours in the day. When a man walks in the day he has the light, but when he is in darkness he stumbles and does not know where he is going."

Any man who has experienced a dangerous profession or anyone who has lived with men so employed can testify to the truth of what Jesus said. The airplane pilot who has lost his nerve and really fears flying is worse than useless, he's dangerous. The deep-sea diver who has developed a fear of water will sooner or later kill himself. When a man becomes afraid of doing what he has trained himself to do, he turns into a shell. He's hollow.

That which is true in the natural realm is far more true in the spiritual. If a man walks with God he is immortal, until his work is done. If he refuses a duty that his spirit tells him is his to perform and refuses out of fear, he walks in the most terrible kind of darkness.

Jesus continued. "Lazarus is asleep, it is necessary that I go wake him."

The disciples were delighted. "Lord, if he's fallen asleep he's getting well. Let's stay here."

Then He told them plainly, "Lazarus is dead. I'm glad that he is dead for I can show you something now that will enable you to believe."

One of the disciples, Thomas, expressed the thoughts of all. "Let's go. That way we can all die together."

When Jesus got to Bethany, Lazarus had been in the grave four days. The wake was still in progress. Bethany was so close to Jerusalem, that many friends of the family were with the two sisters to share in their sorrow. Martha got word that Jesus was finally coming and she left her home and slipped away to greet Him. She had some unkind things to say to Him, and she didn't want to say them in public.

"Lord, why didn't You come? If You had been here my brother would still be alive. I know that whatever You ask of God, God does. You could have asked for my brother's life."

Jesus answered, "Your brother will rise again."

"Yes, Lord, I know about the resurrection in the last days, but that's not a great deal of comfort right now."

"Martha, I am the resurrection and the life." (She missed the tense in the verb, not "I will be," but "I am.") "Whoever believes into (*eis*, Greek) Me is still living and will not taste death."

Paul the Apostle elaborates on this in the fifteenth chapter of First Corinthians. He argues that there are several kinds of bodies, and people who are "in Christ" go on living regardless of what happens to their terrestrial form.

Jesus continued, "Martha, do you believe this?"

She avoided a direct contradiction. "Yes, Lord, You are the Christ, the son of God, the One who was promised, the One who is coming into the world." She was still using the wrong tense.

When she had rebuked Him, she went back to the house and told her sister quietly that the Teacher was in town and was sending for her. Mary rose quickly and went out. Her friends thought she was going to the tomb to weep there, so they followed her.

When Mary reached Jesus she gave Him the same rebuke. "Lord, if only You'd have come. Lazarus would still be alive." She fell at His feet weeping.

Jesus asked her to show Him where they had placed Lazarus. As they walked toward the grave they were followed by the friends of the sisters, and the same bitterness toward Jesus was reflected in their attitude. "Certainly someone who could give sight to a man born blind could have kept Lazarus alive."

This part of the scene is described by the shortest verse in the English Bible. "Jesus wept." If we assume the perspective of Jesus in the story, the reason for His tears was probably the complete and total lack of faith demonstrated by all those around Him. Not only a lack of faith in Him, but a lack of faith in God and in the continuing life that He promised through the prophets. Tears are appropriate at a funeral, no one likes separation from loved ones, but years later the apostle Paul reminded believers that "we have no reason to grieve as do those who have no hope."

Tombs in those days were frequently caves, natural or artificial, dug into the side of a hill and surrounded by a garden. A stone was cut in the shape of a wagon wheel and rolled across the mouth of the cave whenever a body was added to those already buried inside.

Jesus stood in front of the cave and ordered the stone rolled back.

Martha objected. "Lord, he's been dead for four days. If they roll away the stone, the whole place will stink."

It is hard to think of any sentence that would have conveyed a more complete lack of faith.

Jesus answered her, "Martha, didn't I say that if you would believe, you would see the glory of God?"

They took away the stone, and Jesus lifted up His eyes and prayed. "Father, I thank You that You have already heard Me. I know that You always hear Me. I'm praying to You out loud so that these people standing here will know that it is You who is working through Me." Then in a loud voice He cried out: "Lazarus, come out of there."

The text says that Lazarus hopped out as best he could, hobbled as he was by the Jewish burial garments. Jesus said, "Unwrap him and let him go."

Many years ago, there was a famous atheist named Ingersoll who had a lecture in which he "debunked" this story. He claimed that it was a "frameup" between Lazarus, Jesus and the two sisters. The sisters put Lazarus away with food and water to fake the whole thing. Mr. Ingersoll apparently was able to figure something out at a great distance that the enemies of Jesus who were on the scene would have loved to have been able to believe. The temple leaders knew too much about Jewish funerals, Jewish burial customs, and too much about the character of the people involved to believe in a fake. If they could have shown it to be faked, they would have been delighted. Apparently they couldn't, for in the ensuing conversation in the temple among the leaders, there is no question as to the authenticity of the miracle; quite the contrary. They agreed to murder Jesus because if He could raise the dead, the whole world would follow Him. It would mean the end of their power. The resurrection of Lazarus sealed the death warrant against Jesus planned by the religious leaders of His time.

One of Mr. Ingersoll's points was that the cry of Jesus shows collusion. Jesus said, "Lazarus, come forth." If there had been no collusion, "Come forth" would have been enough. The use of name was to show Lazarus that the audience had gathered and it was time for him to come out.

From my father, Dr. Harry Rimmer, I heard a story about Mr. Ingersoll and his observation regarding Lazarus. It seems that on one occasion, Mr. Ingersoll was giving his lecture in a small Canadian town where the local inhabitants had been gathered into the schoolhouse to hear him. When he got to this point he asked his question dramatically.

"If there was not collusion, why did Jesus say, 'Lazarus, come forth' instead of 'come forth'?"

A farmer in the back of the schoolroom raised his hand for permission to speak. When it was granted, he stood up and answered Ingersoll. "If Jesus had said, 'come forth' he'd of had the whole graveyard. He only wanted Lazarus."

Amen, brother.

He conquered the eternal night
By the strength of the Son
And returned to the light.
A second chance, a second life,
But was it worth the dying twice?

Pontius Pilate

We have now reached what may be the most fascinating portrait in our story, the picture of Pontius Pilate, procurator of Judea. There is a great deal of myth connected with this man. Stories concerning the ending of his life are particularly unreliable. The post-crucifixion fate of Pilate was subject to conjecture by many early writers, and the stories tend to be contradictory. The very early history of the man is also open to some question. The strongest theory is that he was the son of a prostitute by a man important to the Roman Empire. Because of his mother, he was born a slave, but gained his freedom through force of arms and ruthlessness.

Information concerning his life during the time of Jesus is much more reliable. He had risen to a place of power, and secular sources took note of him. That he was brutal and good at his profession can be safely deduced from his position. Rome assigned procuratorships on the basis of graft, and there were many who were quite incompetent. Such incompetents were kept close to Rome where they could be given help. Graft was involved in Pilate's assignment, that was S.O.P. (standing operational procedure), but in his case, competence was also taken into consideration. Judea was the source of a great deal of expense to Rome. It was possibly the most troublesome of the conquered areas, and neither the senate nor Caesar would risk sending a man to rule it who could not handle himself.

Pilate's residence in Palestine was at Caesarea. He would have preferred Jerusalem, and on one occasion he tried to move his troops and his household into the city. Because the emblazoned standards of the Roman legions were idols in the eyes of the Jews, riots ensued. The Jews won this skirmish by appealing to Caesar. By command of Rome, all blatantly idolatrous standards were removed from Jerusalem. Pilate moved his headquarters back to Caesarea.

Later, Pilate evened the score. The incident is referred to in the thirteenth chapter of the Gospel of Luke, where some Jews complain to Jesus about Pilate. They accuse Pilate of mixing "the blood of the Galileans with the blood of their sacrifices."

It seems to have happened like this. Pilate ordered some legionaires to dress like Jews and go to the temple and join in a Jewish ceremony. Because a large number of Galileans had come to Jerusalem for this particular ceremonial feast, strangers were not particularly noticeable and the soldiers with their weapons hidden under their robes could join the throng without arousing suspicion.

As the feast began, Pilate had a pig thrown over the wall of the temple court into the midst of the worshipers. A riot ensued as the Jews began to go after their tormentors. Too many men in the crowd were disguised Romans. There was a slaughter. When Pilate was through, the temple courtyard was a scene of terrible carnage.

The hatred between the temple leadership and Pilate was thorough and complete. It is significant that great as it was, the Sanhedrin's hatred of Jesus was even greater. They feared the power of God more than they hated Rome.

After a sham trial in the house of the high priest, the Jewish leadership took Jesus to the praetorium at the first light of dawn. Pilate was there because of the Passover. This annual Jewish feast brought the faithful from all over the world, and for this occasion the population of Jerusalem could be increased by as many as a million people. The presence of these additional, and very zealous Jews increased the possibility of civil disorder. So during each Passover, Pilate left his headquarters at Caesarea, and with at least a cohort, a tenth of a Roman legion, he moved into the Roman buildings in Jerusalem. He stayed there until the Passover feast was finished and the population had returned to normal size.

At the time of our story, Pilate was expecting trouble of some kind. Therefore it was no surprise when the centurion on duty woke him very early on the morning of the day before the Passover to tell him that there was a delegation of Jews outside. They wanted to see the procurator. Pilate knew enough Jewish custom to know that the Pharisees would not enter a Gentile building. Their law would make them "unclean" by so doing, and they would not be qualified to keep the Passover feast in that condition. He ordered the centurion to pick a few of the legionaires who were on watch, and together with them, to accompany him out to talk to the waiting Jews. Whatever it was that the Jews wanted, Pilate was against it before they asked.

The scene was dramatic. On one side stood Pilate, the professional soldier and ruthless military governor of the area, together with his armed soldiers. They were tough men all, or they wouldn't have been assigned to the Judean area. On the other side, the leaders of the temple stood. Their phylacteries were in place, their beautiful religious robes shone with their gold thread in the light of the dawn. There was hatred in their eyes and murder in their hearts.

Pilate spoke first. "What do you Jews want at this ungodly hour?"

The Jewish spokesman pointed to the peasant standing between the two antagonistic groups. It was Jesus, bruised and bleeding. He'd been beaten all night. Pilate spoke again. "What are you accusing this man of doing?"

They didn't want to answer. When Rome took over a province they tried to leave the local government in charge, but Caesar's emissaries always took away two privileges. They kept for Rome the right of capital punishment, and the right of taxation. The Sanhedrin, the Jewish council was granted the right of capital punishment by Mosaic law and by custom. The Jews resented Rome taking that "right" away from them. If they could get Pilate to crucify Jesus on their say so, they would have retrieved tacitly what they felt was theirs anyway. They weren't going to say any more than they had to say.

"If this man were not a criminal, we wouldn't have brought him to you."

Pilate could see their game, and he wasn't about to cooperate. "You've got laws, and you've got courts. Punish him yourselves." He signaled to his soldiers and started back to the praetorium.

The Pharisees stopped him. "Just a moment. You've taken the right of capital punishment away from us. You'll have to do it yourself. It is not right under your law for us to put him to death."

When they conceded their inferior position, Pilate signaled to the centurion to bring Jesus and went back into the praetorium. This building had soldiers' quarters on the main floor and a large room on the second floor where courts of various kinds were held. The second floor room had a porch on it, and through the openings to the porch, Pilate could see the Jews standing below, and far enough away from his building so they wouldn't get "dirty." Pilate could never understand the religious mind. Those men would keep the letter of their Law, they wouldn't have anything unlawful to do with a Gentile, but they didn't mind plotting the murder of the man they'd spent the night beating. He hated them.

There was one factor in this confrontation that was on Pilate's side, and he could see it immediately. Time was on his side. If it had not been, the temple leaders wouldn't have come to the praetorium at the first light of dawn. There were two possible reasons for haste. The first was that the Jews wouldn't want a man crucified on the Passover. They would want to be sure the job was done by sunset when the Jewish day started. The second possible reason was that this man had friends and a large following. If this were true the Jews would want him out of the way before his Hebrew followers knew what was going on. This second possibility had some danger in it. Pilate would frustrate the Jews if he could, but if this Galilean before him were really involved in some kind of rebellion, Pilate would have to be careful. Rome would tolerate almost anything; bribery, corruption of any description, dissipation, name it and it was licensed. Everything, that is, except insurrection. If this man before him had been involved in any kind of conspiracy, Pilate wouldn't be in a position to play around. The Galilean would have to go.

Pilate's first question showed his concern. "Are you the king of the Jews?"

Jesus answered, as He often did, with another question "Is this your idea, or are you just quoting someone else?" With this, the focal point of the conversation between Pilate and Jesus began to shift. The fate of Jesus was already decided, He knew what was going to happen to Him, and He knew why it was going to happen. He was ready for it. But what was Pilate's relationship to his creator? If Jesus could bring Pilate around to a frame of mind that would make faith possible at some later date, the interview would be successful.

Pilate resented the question. "Listen, if the situation were reversed, if a thousand Jews conquered and controlled a million Romans, do you think for one minute that one Roman would turn another Roman over to a Jewish court? Those men hate my guts. What in the world have you done that they would turn you over to me?"

"Put your mind to rest as to the political problem. My kingdom is not this-worldly. It belongs in the next world. If I had any political ambitions I wouldn't be here. I have many servants among the Hebrews and they would have fought the Jews to keep Me from being handed over to you. My kingship is in the next world."

Pilate wasn't quite satisfied. "You are a king then?"

"You keep coming back to the political issue and to the problem of worldly power. That isn't what is on trial here. I was born for a different reason and for this reason I have come into the world. I have come to bear witness to the truth. Everyone who is in touch with reality, everyone who can listen to the truth, listens to Me."

Pilate studied Jesus for a moment. Rapport was building. Most men brought before a procurator facing possible crucifixion were on their face on the floor screaming for mercy. There was a dignity and self-possession about this man that was impressive.

Finally Pilate spoke again. He'd thought the thing through. "What is truth." This is usually followed by a question mark. I think it is wrong to take it as a question. It is a value judgment. It could read, "What is truth worth?"

Pilate had risen to a position of tremendous power. He had gotten there by lying, cheating, bribing and killing. This man who claimed to be truth was poverty-stricken, for the moment friendless, tortured and about to be crucified.

Pilate could see no value to truth, and in terms of this world, Pilate was right.

Because of a desire to frustrate the Jews and a growing respect for Jesus, the Roman wanted to end this if he could. He condescended to walk downstairs and back out to where the temple leaders were waiting. He had thought of an "out."

His manner was conciliatory. "I've talked to this Jesus. I just don't see anything criminal about him. He keeps talking about the next world." He paused for a moment. This wasn't going over too well. "We've had a kind of a custom for the last few years. The procurator releases someone from prison at your request at Passover time." With a deprecating gesture he added "What say, I let go of 'The King of the Jews'?"

There were men in that Roman prison who were valuable to Israel. They were loyal to their people, and they could be of value to the nation and to the resistance against Rome if they could be set free. To have requested such a man would have given dignity to the death of Jesus. The only way they could increase their show of contempt for the Galilean was to ask for the freedom of someone who meant nothing. They picked the lowest thing that came to mind. A recently convicted thief.

"We'll take Barabbas."

Pilate was stunned. He went back to the praetorium and ordered the scourging of Jesus. It wasn't that he'd changed sides, it was just that he'd seen the unbelievable hatred in the eyes of the religious leaders and he knew he'd have to do something. Maybe if he scourged Jesus, they'd let him go, but they wouldn't let him go entirely unmolested.

This kind of reasoning sometimes works. If a contemporary illustration may be permitted, it can shed a little light on Pilate's thinking. At one time in my father's life he was a prize fighter. After the close of this career he worked occasionally as a referee. One night, many years ago, he was asked to referee some inter-service boxing matches at the Presidio in San Francisco. The evening's card started with a three rounder between a sailor and a soldier. It was obvious from the beginning of the fight that the soldier knew a great deal more about boxing than the sailor did. It was anything but an even fight, and the sailor was getting hurt. The noise-filled room was jammed with half-drunken servicemen, and when dad stopped the fight, there was an instant and ominous silence.

A master sergeant sitting ringside got up out of his chair and came over to the ring. He had no way of knowing that the referee was the ex-welterweight champ. The sergeant pulled

the cigar out of his mouth and put his face between the ropes, while he yelled, "We came
here to see some blood."

Dad said he knew he'd have to make it
good, he'd only get one shot. With the flick of
his hand that only the professional fighter can
master, he spread the sergeant's nose evenly all
over his fat face.

"There's some blood."

The crowd laughed, the tension eased and
the next two fighters were called to the ring.

Pilate's plan could have been, "I'll beat
him up and they'll let him go."

The scourging was a terrible thing. The
victim's hands and feet were tied to a post
about six inches high so that his back was ex-
posed, "U" shaped. Josephus, the historian,
says that in 70 A.D., when Titus took Jerusalem,
he scourged and crucified ten thousand Hebrews of military age. According to the ancient
record only one in ten was crucified. The other
nine couldn't be nailed to the cross because the
whip, frequently embellished with pieces of
metal, had cut the victim into two pieces.

Outside the praetorium the Jews realized
that Pilate was stalling. They passed the word
to bring to the praetorium people who were
pro-temple. Their religion was big business
and there were plenty of men around whose
income had been hurt by Jesus' cleansing the

temple. Such men packed the area around the praetorium so that the friends of Jesus couldn't get close to the building.

When the Romans were through scourging Jesus, they ridiculed Him. They took one of the king's robes, purple and rich in texture, and mimicked the king's headpiece with a crown of thorns. Pilate took Jesus out on the porch of the praetorium where the crowd could see. Jesus stood beaten almost to death, in a pool of His own blood and in agony. Pilate thought that would be enough for anyone.

"This is no criminal. And look at him. Let's call it off and all go home."

Pilate did not count on the implacable nature of the religious mind. The temple crowd screamed, "Crucify him, crucify him."

It turned Pilate's stomach. He'd had all he could take. "You crucify him yourselves. I find nothing wrong with him."

He turned away in disgust, but the temple leaders called him back. They had to come up with the one accusation they had hoped they would never have to make. They made it. "We have a law, and by that law Jesus must die. He says that his father, his immediate father is God."

Pilate's blood ran cold. He had been raised within the Roman framework of Greek religious beliefs, and probably like most practical men of his day he dismissed these beliefs as untrue but politically useful. The Greek-Roman religions were full of stories of men who were the product of intercourse between a god and a human. All his life he'd given such tales little credibility. After all, Tiberius Caesar was a god, and Pilate knew him well. Tiberius was clearly very human. Pilate bowed to Tiberius because Pilate was Roman, not because he was religious.

This man Jesus was different. Suddenly Pilate had an explanation for the terrible quietness and composure of Jesus under torture. Did this man act like he acted, this Jesus, because he was half god and half man?

(In passing, there is one observation that should be made concerning the orthodox view of the nature of Jesus. This observation is based on the reaction of Pilate to this information concerning the claim of Jesus. Pilate could see that the Jews would have no grounds under their own law to continue the miserable business if either Jesus or his mother had named any man as the biological father of Jesus. Those of us who have had the questionable privilege of witnessing torture are aware of the horror that is thereby induced. Pilate had witnessed plenty, and he knew that in due time any man will say anything. All Jesus would have had to do was to say that Joseph, who had been the legal husband of his mother, was his father, and the whole process would have stopped.)

Pilate left the porch and went back into the courtroom with Jesus. His face was ashen. "Where are You from?"

Pilate knew Jesus was Galilean, he could have told that by the accent if by no other means, and he knew where Galilee was. Geography was not on Pilate's mind. What he wanted to know, and what he meant by his question had nothing to do with Palestine, but he couldn't bring himself to ask, "Are you from another world?"

Jesus stared at him and said nothing.

The procurator came apart. "You won't even speak to me, to ME! Don't you know I have the power to let you go, or the power to nail you up to dry? Open your mouth."

Jesus answered, "You don't have any real power. You are doing the will of your superiors and carrying out your duties. The real culprits are those who turned Me over to you and put you in this dilemma."

That was more than Pilate could take. He'd had Jesus brutally beaten after admitting his ignorance of any crime. He had treated Jesus as he would not have dared to treat Him had Jesus been a Roman citizen. Also Pilate knew something of the psychotic hatred that a man has toward someone who has tortured him. Instead of displaying His hatred, Jesus was apologizing to Pilate for Pilate's behavior.

Pilate ran back out of the praetorium where he could face the Jews. There was a stony silence while they waited for him to speak. "I won't crucify that man for you bunch of bloodthirsty religious bastards for all the gold in Palestine!"

The professional politician, even one that is Roman and ruthless, is no match for the ecclesiastical politician. The religious man lives in the world of abstractions and he has not had to spend time or the energy on the practical. In the world of conniving, he can be one jump ahead. The high priest was one up on Pilate.

"This man, Jesus, whom you are now protecting calls Himself a King, and any man who calls himself a king sets himself against Caesar. Shall we call this matter to the attention of Rome?"

That hurt. The exact year in which this took place has not been determined, but it was close to the end of the reign of Tiberius. If Caligula had taken the throne, Rome was in real trouble, for it was correctly rumored that Caligula was insane and the senate had lost much of its power. But with either man on the throne, Pilate was in trouble. If the Jews sent a delegation to Rome charging Pilate with aiding and abetting insurrection he might get a fair enough trial to escape with his life, but it would cost him all he had and would probably end his career. Here was his choice: All he had struggled to attain, or the life of a Galilean peasant named Jesus, a man who might be of supernatural origin.

The drives, the values, the acquisitions of a lifetime are not easily reversed. Pilate gave in to the practical, but there was going to be a price that the Jews were going to have to pay. They were in a hurry, the day was waning, and they would want no man on the cross after sunset.

Pilate took his time, sauntered back up to the court and brought Jesus back downstairs to the street level. Pilate seated himself at the court of the pavement. (In our culture we would call it a small claims court. Usually it was presided over by a Roman noncommissioned officer who settled small disputes, or sent important ones to the courtroom above him.) The text says it was the sixth hour. The Romans started time with sunrise, so it was about noon. The Jews started the day with sunset, so they had six hours in which to get Jesus on the cross and down again. They were in a hurry. Pilate wasn't.

He seated himself comfortably, crossed his legs and pointed to the bruised and beaten Jesus, who had been forced to stand beside him. "Behold your king."

The temple leaders screamed at him: "Crucify him."

They were going to have to say more than that before Pilate would let them have their way with Jesus. They had never openly admitted servitude to Rome. Pilate pointed at Jesus again: "Shall I crucify your king?"

There was silence. Time was running out and the Jews could not wait very much longer. They were going to get their way but there was a price. After consultation, they decided to pay it.

Through clenched teeth the Jews forced out the words, "We have no king but Caesar."

Pilate had gotten all he could get. He nodded to the centurion: "Crucify him."

The Jews thought they had won, but Pilate had one more trick up his sleeve. He called in a sign painter and told him what he wanted. Over the head of Jesus as He was nailed to the cross a sign was fixed. Pilate had it printed in the three languages common to the area so that any man who walked by could read it. In Hebrew, Latin and Greek it said: "The King of the Jews."

The high priests heard about it and protested. They sent still another delegation to Pilate. "You had no business saying that. Tell the truth, say 'This man said He was the king of the Jews.'"

Pilate smiled at them coldly and said, "*Gegrapha, gegrapha.*" It has been translated down through the ages, "What I have written, I have written." This is not the only way to translate it. The verb is in the first person singular, perfect, indicative, active. When two perfect tenses are in juxtaposition, the grammarians will let us translate the second perfect tense as a future. I think Pilate was giving his testimony to Jesus. Jesus had won the man, for Pilate said: "What I wrote will forever stand written."

It is a matter of personal conjecture for which I have no evidence outside the story. My guess is that after the resurrection, Jesus was Pilate's King too.

They brought Him to me
For what their power could not do.
Only I had the right
To free or condemn
This bruised and bloodied
King of the Jews.

His fate in my hands
But still His silent strength remained.
He knew I was trapped
By their self-righteous hate
And His precious blood spilled
As their loss, but my gain.

Simon Peter

One of our first mentioned witnesses to Jesus was Simon Peter: The man who would someday be called "the rock." He appears in the Gospel of John five more times. Except for his last appearance, a great deal can be learned about the man, and about his relationship to Jesus by assuming, correctly I think, that every time he opened his mouth he said the wrong thing.

The assumption that Jesus had twelve disciples is only partly correct. The text says that He chose twelve from among His disciples. Early in His ministry, Jesus had hundreds. At the crucifixion He stood alone. One of the first of the winnowing processes took place in the sixth chapter.

Jesus had fed the multitude and there is nothing like free food to draw a crowd. When He spoke the following Sabbath in the synagogue at Capernaum the building was packed with His disciples. They wanted a continuation of the concept that they had seen. They had biblical grounds for it. When Moses led their forefathers out of the wilderness, God provided bread from heaven, and a rock that supplied water. If Jesus was the promised Messiah, it was right in their eyes that this relationship should be re-established. They wanted more bread.

In an argument that must have been painful to Jesus, He tried to turn their minds from earthly bread to heavenly. "I am the bread, which comes down from heaven. Your fathers ate the manna and they died. He who is eating my flesh, and drinking my blood, shall never taste death."

He was trying, as did Paul years later, to get them to see that the historic record of the Israelites was loaded with spiritual significance. The physical bread of the wilderness experience was a prophetic figure for the spiritual bread. The physical bread sustained physical life temporarily. The Israelites ate it, but in the end they died physically. Jesus is saying that His body and blood (looking forward to the symbolism of communion) sustains spiritual life. It sustains it in such a manner that the partaker will never taste spiritual death, or complete separation from God.

The response of the disciples was disappointing. "This is stupid. How can we eat His flesh and drink His blood?" The text says that many withdrew and went about with Him no more. As a matter of fact, that sermon emptied the synagogue. When Jesus was through preaching, there were only twelve men remaining.

He turned to them. "Don't you want to leave also?"

Peter answered: "Lord, where would we go? You alone have the words of real life. We know that You are come from God."

Jesus answered in a veiled way. "I chose you, and one of you is a devil." Jesus is making the point that contrary to what Peter implied, they were not following Him because of their own inner resources. If they were, Judas would not be among them. The twelve were there because Jesus had asked the Father for them and they were being given the insight and motivation to stay. The disciples didn't have the spiritual resources to follow Jesus in their own strength.

Peter shows up again in the thirteenth chapter. Jesus washed the feet of the twelve, including Judas, and talked to them about their relationship to Him and to each other. Peter was impressed and he swore undying loyalty to Jesus. "Lord, I will follow You anywhere, I will never betray You. I will die for You."

Peter was wrong again. Jesus said, "That's what you think. I'll tell you something, Peter; before the cock crows to signal the dawn, you will have denied me three times."

In his heart, Peter swore to himself that this would never happen and so at the arrest of Jesus by the temple soldiers, in the eighteenth chapter, it was Peter who tried to put up a defense. He drew his sword and charged. He was a fisherman, not a soldier. All he got for his effort was the ear of a slave named Malchus, and a rebuke from Jesus.

After the soldiers had arrested Jesus, they took Him to Annas, the Jewish high priest. Jewish custom provided that when a man was appointed high priest, he held that office until death. Annas was the oldest high priest, and so in the eyes of the Jews he was the real high priest and Jesus was taken to him first. The Romans appointed high priests as they saw fit. At the time of the trial of Jesus, Caiaphas, the son-in-law of Annas, was the high priest by Roman appointment. The Jews went along with the act but they didn't change their custom. This is why, in the text, both Annas and Caiaphas are called high priest. Both men lived in a huge home in Jerusalem. It was walled and defended by temple soldiers. It was to this house that the soldiers took Jesus after His arrest.

Peter followed at a distance. Because John, the writer of the Gospel, was a member of a wealthy family, he was known to the household of Annas and Caiaphas. He was permitted to accompany the group that brought in Jesus. Peter, more distinctly Galilean, felt out of place and he followed too far behind to enter the courtyard when the crowd did. The gate was closed and he was outside.

From the porch where John was standing near Jesus, he could look down over the wall and see that Peter was locked outside. He found a maid, one of the household servants and sent her to open the gate and let Peter into the courtyard.

When Peter said, "Thank you" to the girl for opening the gate, he said it with a Galilean accent. The maid asked, "Hey, you're one of the nuts who follow that Galilean, aren't you?"

Many a strong man can brace himself to resist force and die. The same man, caught unaware, can be demolished by ridicule. Peter opened his mouth and said the wrong thing yet again. "I am not!"

It was early spring, and the evenings were cold. The soldiers stationed at the home of the high priest had built a fire in the courtyard. They, together with some of the off-duty servants of the household, were standing around glowing charcoal, warming themselves. Peter wandered over and joined the group as inconspicuously as possible. It wasn't inconspicuous enough. A couple of the men were studying him.

One of them spoke up, "Aren't you a follower of the Galilean?"

This time Peter answered with a little heat. "No. Don't be ridiculous."

From the balcony above, the sounds that accompanied the "questioning" of Jesus drifted down into the courtyard. The men holding Jesus were slapping Him around and laughing at Him. An hour went by and then one of the soldiers who had been watching Peter spoke up. "I know you. I'm the cousin of Malchus whose ear you hacked off. You were in the garden with the Galilean when we picked Him up."

Peter swore at him. "Don't any of you accuse me of being with Him again."

The attention of the group was diverted by the sight of Jesus being led to the confrontation with Pilate. As Jesus reached the stairs that led down from the balcony, He could see those who were gathered around the fire. This included Peter, and their eyes met.

At that moment the cock crowed in the distance, and the prophecy of Jesus concerning the unfaithfulness of Peter came flooding back into Peter's mind. At that moment, Peter counted himself outside of the kingdom of God.

Evidence for Peter's reasoning is found in the words of Jesus after the resurrection. "Go tell My disciples and Peter that I have risen."

He said "and Peter," because He knew that Peter no longer numbered himself among the disciples. Had this been the opinion of Jesus also, He would have said, "Go tell the disciples and Simon." Simon didn't mean "rock," and Jesus was trying to tell Peter that he was still "in" by using the name that would someday be true. In effect He said, "Tell the rock I'm alive."

Peter's final appearance is in the closing chapter of the book. He is still hanging back, self-incriminated and feeling miserable. He believes in the resurrection, he has testified to it, but he does not any longer believe in himself. His self-acceptance was demolished by what he had done and his depression was apparent to his friends.

When Peter said, "I'm going fishing," his friends went with him. A man so depressed should not be left alone. The fishing trip did nothing to enliven the party. They worked all night casting and dragging in their nets. No fish were caught.

As the dawn began to break, they were close to shore. They saw a man on the beach bending over a fire. He turned and looked at them. In a moment He stood and called out, "Any fish?"

"Nope. Not a one."

"Cast your net on the right side of your boat and you'll get fish."

The men looked at each other and shrugged, so what's one more toss. They heaved the net and started it back to the boat. It was anything but empty, it was alive with struggling fish. John was a Hebrew. He counted them and he remembered, "one hundred and fifty-three."

The disciples looked down on the teeming fish and began to think, but it was John who said it first. "That man on the beach is the Lord. It's got to be."

Impetuous as always, Simon Peter grabbed his robe and jumped into the sea, making for the shore. When he got there, he stood and looked at the man. Peter was reinstated but it had to be proven to Peter. Jesus started the procedure by making a request.

"Bring Me some of the fish you just caught." He didn't need them, fish were already on the fire, but He wanted to ask a favor. People don't ask favors politely of those whom they scorn. Peter did as he was asked immediately.

Jesus was doing one thing more. It was for all the disciples, including Peter. They had a visual, physical image of a man. This had to be fuzzed. Years later, the apostle Paul put it neatly. "We knew Jesus once as just a man, but from now on we know Him that way no more." The "humiliation of the incarnation" was passing. The image of "The Son of man" was fading. In its place, in the minds of the disciples there was growing, "Jesus, God's Son, Lord and Savior." This image was the combination of what He had said and what He had done: the words and the works that the Father had given Him to do. There is strong indication that in His post-resurrection appearances He never appeared twice looking exactly as He had looked before.

When the boat had been brought to shore and the men were standing on the beach, Jesus spoke again. "Come and have some breakfast."

They sat down and Jesus waited on them, serving them fish and bread. The disciples stole glances at each other affirming what each believed separately. They didn't need to ask; this was the Lord.

After breakfast Jesus spoke to Simon Peter. He went back to the old name. "Simon, son of John, do you love Me more than these?" He pointed to the fishing boat and equipment.

Simon answered miserably. He probably was remembering the time when Jesus was talking to the rich young ruler and Peter had bragged about leaving everything for Jesus. If he had, where did he get the boat? "Yes, Lord, you know I love You."

"Feed My lambs."

There was a moment's silence and Jesus spoke again. "Simon, son of John, do you love Me?"

"Yes, Lord, You know that I love You."

"Take care of My sheep."

After another silence, Jesus asked again: "Simon, do you love Me?"

Simon Peter was upset. The significance of what Jesus was doing didn't dawn on him at that moment but when he looked back on it he would understand. Jesus was giving him a chance to state his love, one time for every time

Peter had denied he knew Him. He didn't get the point just then and he spoke impatiently.

"Please, Lord, please. You know everything. You know that I love You."

"Feed My sheep."

Jesus had made a promise to Peter concerning a change in his personality. Peter had no way of knowing at the time that the promise was given, that the promised change was dependent upon a subsequent work of God. The work that God would do through His Spirit in placing within Peter a small portion of the nature of Jesus Christ. Jesus spoke to Peter once more, to give him an assurance that what Jesus had prophesied would come true: Peter would be changed.

"Peter, listen. As a young man you've been headstrong and independent. You've dressed as you pleased and gone where you wished. This is going to change. The day is coming when you will stretch out your hands and men will bind you and take you where you do not want to go, but you'll go."

The text says that Jesus was prophesying by what death Peter would glorify God. That day came and Peter died, steady as a rock.

Three times I denied Him
Denied His love
Denied His pain
And even my faith—
My very self—
Denied in shame.
But still He called me
And with His love
My own did reinstate.

Again in threes
He placed in me
A Rock, A Task, A Fate.